DOWN AND OUT IN
PHILADELPHIA
AND NEW YORK

GARRET GODWIN

Author's Tranquility Press
MARIETTA, GEORGIA

Garret Godwin/Author's Tranquility Press
2706 Station Club Drive SW
Marietta, GA 30060
www.authorstranquilitypress.com

Ordering Information:
Quantity sales. Special discounts are available on quantity purchases by corporations, associations, and others. For details, contact the "Special Sales Department" at the address above.

Down and Out Philadelphia and New York/Garret Godwin
Hardback: 978-1-959197-29-4
Paperback: 978-1-959197-40-9
eBook: 978-1-959197-41-6

This book is dedicated to George Orwell, a.k.a. Eric Blair, the visionary who died before his time.

CONTENTS

CHAPTER

1

When starting out in life, one is somehow immune to the environment in which one finds himself. Please let me explain. When one is young, despite whatever circumstances he finds himself in, there is hope that the future will be better. He works to position himself in society, in short, to be successful and live a happy, rewarding life. Of course, not everyone succeeds in this. Extraneous forces like luck, fate, geography and the whims of other people come into play. Nevertheless, while character is still being formed, the exuberance of youth surmounts all of these obstacles.

While I was a graduate student in English literature, such were my circumstances. Oblivious to my environment, my mind was absorbed in studying the great literature of the past. I had no final destination. My purpose was unclear. I just knew that I loved what I was doing, I loved the genius scholars I was studying with, and I couldn't imagine myself doing anything else.

I proved to be such a good scholar that I was granted a teaching assistantship of four hundred dollars per month. It was the late 1970s, and I had no idea how far four hundred dollars a month would go in a major city like Philadelphia. I had an apartment for a hundred dollars a month, which left me three hundred dollars for all of my other expenses, and I found that I was able to stretch that three hundred dollar and live successfully.

I was living in a section of Philadelphia called Oak Lane. Actually, it was East Oak Lane, because there was also a West Oak Lane. East Oak Lane was predominantly white, whereas West Oak Lane was predominantly black. Within East Oak Lane, there were pockets of Ukrainians, Eastern European Jews, Irish, and students of many different ethnic backgrounds. In the 1930s, it had been a very fashionable part of town, with big Victorian houses lining the tree-shaded streets, and it had the bonus of being close to public transportation. Currently, the subway to downtown was fifty cents. Back then, it was probably a nickel. A dollar a day for the subway amounted to twenty dollars a month. That still left two hundred and eighty dollars for food and miscellaneous expenses.

At the urban university that I was attending, there were "lunch trucks" parked outside all the major buildings. This being Philadelphia, the main food sold was cheese steaks, and they were delicious. Over a foot long, they were an amalgam of thin strips of steak mixed with cheese and sautéed onions. After eating one of them, there was no need to eat again for at least six to eight hours. The other Philadelphia food institution was soft pretzels with mustard. Sometimes they were the desert after a good cheese steak, or for dieters, they were the main meal. Both of these plus a drink could be had for under five dollars. Thus, at maximum, enough food to keep one alive for a month could be had for under one hundred and fifty dollars. That still left one hundred and thirty dollars for miscellaneous expenses.

I had a VW beetle to run around town with. Rarely did I use more than a tank of gas per month. The subway was only several blocks from my apartment.

I had several friends in town that I would visit occasionally. One was a fellow graduate English student like myself named Rick. He was also a fellow graduate of the rural university that I had graduated from. Through him, I met a graduate sociology student with whom I would eventually form a lifelong friendship. His name was Max. He was a sociologist of the Marxist persuasion, and his take on everything opened my mind to things that I had never considered before. He was from a working-class family, but he was brilliant and he knew it. He had also received a teaching assistantship from his department and spent most of his time at the university.

His mission in life was to revolutionize the world, and my mission was to understand the human condition. Together, we made quite a team. Sometimes we would stay up until the late hours of the morning discussing sociology and literature. We were also both single males in our twenties with testosterone to spare. Chasing women was also part of our social agenda. There were many gorgeous women all over Philadelphia, and a team worked much better than a lone male on the prowl. We both knew this, and our individual skills complemented each other very well.

My routine varied from day to day, depending upon the time of my classes and the classes I taught. Sometimes my classes started at seven o'clock at night and I wouldn't get home until eleven at night. Most nights I was home at five o'clock at night. If I was through studying for the day, I'd call Max and see if he wanted to go out. More often than not he did, and we would hit a local bar and muster up our courage to talk with women. Max was more than an extrovert than I was, and he'd usually instigate the conversation. Once "in," however, I was a valuable ally, as I could pick up quickly on just about any conversation.

There was a bar in Jenkintown, a few miles north of us that we particularly liked to frequent. The name of the place was Jasper's, and it was known as a good student hangout. For some reason, beer just didn't fit the bill at Jasper's, and Max and I developed a taste for tequila. It didn't take many shots of tequila to get quite drunk.

One night, Max got more drunk on tequila than I did, but he wasn't through yet. He walked up to the bar and said to the bartender, "Hey amigo, another round of tequila for my friend and me." The bartender hesitated at first but decided not to cut him off just yet. Max came back to the table with the two tequilas and started staring at two women across the room. He threw his shot into the back of his throat and said, "They look like fair game—let's go."

Max and I got up and walked across the bar, and Max asked them if we could buy them a drink. When they said yes, we sat down next to them and asked the waitress for a round of four tequilas. By the time she got back, Max had already had most of his "target's story. I was still making small talk with my potential future date. The ultimate bad word had already come up in Max's conversation—boyfriend—but Max was drunk and he was determined to go as far as he could possibly go despite this dreadful word. I had already been politely shot down and was just waiting to see what Max's next move would be. It finally dawned on him that this was a losing venture, and as he started to get up he said, "Well, nice talking with you." We walked back to our table somewhat humbled by the experience. We had been "bageled," as in doughnut, as in zero. To be "bageled" was to have exactly zero prospects, and there would be many times when this would be our condition.

CHAPTER

2

One of the beautiful things about being a student is that you are not on a rigid schedule, and you have time to explore your environment and do things that most nine-to-fivers can't do. My studies kept me busy enough, however, that I couldn't go out exploring every day. But when I did, I saw things through the eyes of a fully-grown child. On my first visit to Rittenhouse Square, I thought what a wonderful, quaint little park it was. It was only a square block or so in size, but the way the statues and trees were laid out made it beautiful. This was really the "in" part of the city, where most of the really trendy city-dwellers lived. There was a theater on the north side of the square, and a bar on the east side, while most of the rest of it was lined with tall apartment buildings.

I had found a coffee shop about a block north of Rittenhouse Square to study in. It wasn't exactly a great place to read because it was pretty noisy, but it was a great place to write papers, and writing papers is what being an

English major is all about. Sometimes I would go there with some of my fellow graduate students and we would shoot the breeze for hours. The name of the place was the Alva, and I never knew where the name came from, just that the coffee was good and cheap and the food tolerable and cheap.

A few blocks further up Eighteenth Street one eventually comes to Logan Circle, where the word LOVE is spelled out in a sculpture in the middle of a beautiful fountain. It is situated in a hub where Market Street intersects with the beginning of JFK Boulevard. What detracted from the beauty of the place is that there always seemed to be beggars and the homeless hanging out at the "Circle." It was impossible to stay there for any length of time without being accosted by one of them. They should have been aware of the fact that to a student a quarter was a lot of money. Nevertheless, my heart made me give over to them any extra change I may have had whenever I was approached. Most of them were black and old, and they always seemed to be wearing clothing inappropriate to the season. I always thought what a shame it was that such a beautiful spot should be tarnished by the ever-present specter of poverty.

A few blocks to the west and one or two blocks to the south stands the Free Library of Philadelphia. It is truly a marvel of Greek architecture and a magnificent building. Its white marble columns stand tall, and upon entering it one feels as though he had just entered the Parthenon. I never figured out the secret of how the Free Library kept out the riff-raff, but they were successful at it. I never saw a down-and-out person within the confines of the Free

Library, even though there were a multitude of places inside where such could have hidden.

The only difficulty with the Free Library was that it had so many books from all over the world, it was difficult to find the one you wanted. Even though it used the Dewey Decimal System, with all its floors and wings and being so enormous, it could take hours to find one book. The library of the university that I was attending was half the size of the Free Library, but because of this, it was easy to find the book I needed. Not only was it twice as close to home as the Free Library, but it also had those wonderful lunch trucks parked outside of it, where food could be acquired at almost any hour. For these reasons, I preferred the university library, although if I wanted to be exhilarated by beauty, I would occasionally go to the Free Library.

CHAPTER

3

Geography was always one of my favorite subjects when I was in junior high school. I always loved memorizing the names of rivers and mountain ranges. Since there are no mountains in Philadelphia, I made an extra effort to get to know its rivers. Philadelphia is situated between the Delaware and Schuylkill Rivers just as Manhattan is situated between the East and the Hudson Rivers. The Schuylkill River forms the border of Fairmount Park to the west, and the Delaware forms the border between New Jersey and Pennsylvania on the east. The easier of the two to access was the Schuylkill River. Many times I would drive to a place called Valley Green, the northernmost tip of Fairmount Park. This area of the park is stunningly beautiful, with centuries-old trees bordering the narrowing Schuylkill River. Fairmount Park is the largest inner-city park in the country, and the founding fathers couldn't have planned it better. It is more than twenty miles long, and there are innumerable treasures to be found within its borders.

The grandest part of Fairmount Park is where the Philadelphia Museum of Art and Boat House Row look out over the Schuylkill River. It is one of the most impressive visages of any city in the world. On certain Friday nights, there would be parties in one of the houses on Boat House Row, and they really were a special event. Most of the Boat House Row houses were owned by various universities so their rowing team would have a place to practice. On any given day between May and October, any number of rowing teams could be seen out on the river practicing for some event.

As my first year of graduate studies came to an end, I realized that I loved this city and would probably never want to leave it. In the interest of economics, however, I had to move back into my parents' rural home to find a job and make enough money so that the next year would be easier. Perhaps next fall I could find a larger apartment and have more extra money to spend. Of course, one could never be certain of this.

After my boring three-month stint in rural Pennsylvania, it was time to start looking for an apartment in Philadelphia for the next academic year. My first stop was the bulletin board in the humanities building. As I looked at all of the listings in front of me, a strange notion came over me. Why not live in the heart of the city? After three months, I had enough of the country, and I didn't want to live on the fringe of the city anymore. I wanted to be in the heart of it all. I wanted to experience the hustle-bustle, hear the noise, and become an urbanite. I found an ad that said, "three female law students looking for one more roommate." I gave the number a call, and one of the female law students said I could visit the place that afternoon. The address was 15th and Locust— one block from the Broad Street subway.

When I got there, a small Jewish woman opened the door. She was only five feet tall with jet-black hair and brown eyes. Her name was Susan and she had a pleasant personality. It was an old brownstone three floors high, with two bedrooms on the second floor and two bedrooms on the third floor. My bedroom, if I wanted it, was on the top floor. Classes started tomorrow, so being rather desperate, I said I would take it. My share of the rent was one hundred and fifty dollars a month. I had made it on three hundred dollars a month spending money last year, so I figured I could somehow survive on fifty dollars less a month. Besides, I had managed to save over the summer, and I figured that would go pretty far. I said, "I'll take it."

I didn't meet the other two roommates until I moved in the next day. One was a dark-haired New England girl from Massachusetts—Darcy, and the other was a short, cute, blonde girl from Washington, D.C.—Cathy. Thus, only Susan was a native Philadelphian.

We all got to know one another during that fall semester. All Susan did was study, and she was the least fun. The other two law students studied a lot too, but they also allowed themselves to have some fun. I was most attracted to Darcy, the dark-haired New England girl, but I dared not make a move and destroy the camaraderie of the household. I decided to keep my feelings to myself and see what developed with time.

My routine was the opposite of what I had last year. I got on the subway in center city and commuted north to the mid-north Philadelphia University I was attending. Living in the inner city made me feel like a true city slicker, and it was so much easier to visit all the places downtown that I liked to visit.

I saw that law school was no breeze, but on the other hand, I think my three female roommates began to see that graduate English literature was no cakewalk either. Very few times did we eat a communal meal together. Our various schedules kept us out of the house for most of the day, and most evenings were spent with our different groups of friends.

I had friends who lived on Pine Street, but Max and Rick still lived in East Oak Lane. Between having some friends in the city and some living in the fringe suburbs, I pretty much got all over the city just to meet with my friends. The friend who lived on Pine Street—Harry— was another graduate of the rural university I had attended as an undergraduate. He had two male roommates who were pretty friendly. On occasion, they would hold parties, and my two friends from the northern suburbs would come down and we'd usually get quite drunk. Max would always have girls hanging on him by the end of the evening. He was a true "babe magnet." He could always get a girl; his problem was in keeping her.

Towards the end of the fall semester, I only had three hundred dollars left of the two grand I had made during the summer. It became apparent that I needed another source of income besides my teaching assistantship. I saw on the graduate English bulletin board that there was an opening for a copyeditor for the Journal of the History of Ideas in the philosophy department. The pay was meager, but the work would be intellectually stimulating and I knew I would enjoy the work. I went down to the graduate philosophy headquarters a floor below our own and interviewed for the position with Dr. Wisdom, the editor of the journal. I could tell at once that he liked me, and after fifteen minutes I was offered the job. I could start next week.

Buoyant with the knowledge that I would soon be earning additional money, I was in the mood to celebrate a little bit. I called Max to see if he wanted to go out drinking. He did. We went to Jasper's for happy hour. The bartender remembered Max from "tequila night." "Hey gringo, another tequila?" he asked as he watched Max walk through the door. Max laughed and said, "Hey gringo" back. We sat down at a table near the bar and I told Max about my new gig as copy-editor for a philosophy department journal. He was very happy for me and wished me good luck with it. Max was actually a little bit jealous. He hadn't been able to find additional employment within the university and had to find a job in the real world to supplement his income. His part-time job was at a place called The Center for Aging. I asked him what he did and he told me but I guess it was something that only sociologists can understand because I couldn't understand it.

I reported to Dr. Wisdom on Monday and he showed me what he wanted—check every article for grammar and diction, make sure references were in the correct bibliographic format, and check to make sure that all footnotes were correct. It was an easy job because most of the papers were written by world-famous scholars. Occasionally there would be a mistake, but not enough to justify my wages. I had really landed a plum job, and I tried to show my appreciation to Dr. Wisdom every chance I got. Looking at manuscripts with an editor's eye also helped me in my own studies. I was better at proofreading my own papers and was quicker to catch something that was incorrect.

Some of my fellow English majors were jealous too. Every TA in the department had heard of my gig, and most of them wished they had applied for it. Between my TA, the leftover savings from the summer, and the money from my new gig, I felt like I was rolling in it. I wasn't getting any help from home, but I knew that all of my roommates were. I was proud of the fact that I was making it on my own because I knew that many students my age weren't.

As the end of the semester neared and I was writing my final papers, I knew that some of my papers flashed with a little bit of brilliance that my earlier papers lacked. Maybe some of those papers that I was copyediting had rubbed off on me. I don't know, but I did know that my mind was the better for it.

CHAPTER

C hristmas break 1978 was a very special time for me and my family. I was at the halfway mark in completing my master's degree in English literature, and I was beginning to see the light at the end of the tunnel. I had no idea yet what I wanted to do with it, but the knowledge was there and I was very proud of it. I was well on the road to becoming a serious intellectual, and I was very proud of this fact.

My father and mother were very proud of the progress I was making, and when I told my father about the copyediting job, he seemed to beam with pride. On my meager wages, I was actually able to come home laden with Christmas presents, albeit inexpensive ones. It was a white Christmas that year, and the house was decorated with lights on the outside and a beautiful Christmas tree on the inside.

All the money that I had left over from my summer job went towards the Christmas presents. Not that I had that many people to buy for—only my parents and my sister, but I had gone a little overboard and bought three expensive presents—a chandelier for my parents and a nice, warm winter coat for my sister. After all, I knew I would be O.K. what with my copyediting job and my TA. Besides, I always received great presents from my parents, and for the first time, I felt like I was returning the favor.

Fueled by excess turkey and other Christmas food, I couldn't wait to get back to Philadelphia. I had taken a strong interest in American literature, and I was at a point in my studies now that I could choose a concentration.

When I arrived back in Philadelphia, my three female roommates were already back in school. They welcomed me back with smiles and said they hoped I had a nice Christmas. I replied in the affirmative and headed east towards the Broad Street subway. I was traveling to class in brand new duds, and I felt like the world was my oyster. I carelessly had my left leg sticking out into the center aisle of the subway train. At the Vine Street stop, a black man carrying a bottle of beer in his hand tripped over my leg and he nearly fell down. I was startled and said, "Excuse me." He looked at me with menacing eyes, and I said, "Excuse me" again. At this point, he smashed the top of his beer bottle on one of the seats, leaving a cut glass weapon in his hands. As he said, "What did you say?" I noticed that the train was pulling into my Montgomery Avenue stop. I jumped up in a hurry and ran off the train, not daring to look back. I ran up the steps to the street and finally a block later I looked back. He didn't follow me. I sighed a sigh of relief and began to realize how lucky I'd been to escape without my throat being slit.

This had been my first experience with violence since I had moved to the big city. I sat in the graduate student lounge well into the mid-evening thinking about the incident. Had I said excuse me loud enough for him to hear? Maybe he was so drunk that he actually thought that I was trying to trip him. At least he didn't call me "Honky." I made a mental note to myself that I would never leave my legs sticking out in the aisle on the subway again.

That spring semester of 1979 I learned a lot about how to survive in the big city on a small budget. If being a poor graduate student for a number of years doesn't teach you thrift, nothing will. One learns the difference between fixed costs and variable costs. Rent, the subway, and books are fixed costs, while food, clothing, and entertainment are variable costs. One might think that books would be a variable cost, but in fact, books always ran about fifty dollars a semester. The sum total of all the books' prices tended to average out. It was uncanny, but that average was always fifty dollars give or take a few bucks.

It was in the middle of this spring semester that something extraordinary happened. A nuclear power plant called Three Mile Island had a near meltdown. My parents' home was only twenty or so miles away. I watched the news reports and heard that everyone within ten miles of the plant was being evacuated. I was very concerned about my parents and my sister. I called them every night during the crisis.

There were news agencies from all over the world congregated at Three Mile Island waiting to see how bad the accident was. I counted my blessings that I was nowhere near the place. I couldn't think about it too long though, because my studies had to come first, and my classes were becoming difficult. At least my parents were out of the ten-mile danger zone, and they probably weren't in any danger.

It was April 1979, and the weather was beautiful. I found time to visit all the important landmarks in Philadelphia like Independence Mall, the Philadelphia Museum of Art, Washington Square, and Penn's Landing on the Delaware River. I was starting to date Elsie, a fellow graduate English student. She was probably the smartest student in the English department. She was a beautiful, black-haired, blue-eyed beauty. Her parents lived in the Jewish section of Elkin's Park, and they pretended to like me. Elsie and I both had one more year to go to get our graduate English degrees. For a Goyim, she respected me, which I later learned was quite a compliment. We planned to live together our last year of studies to save money.

The TMI accident was actually a stroke of good luck for me for it provided me with my next summer job. The Nuclear Regulatory Commission needed canvassers to find out if there were any lingering illnesses caused by the accident. Students were hired to go door-to-door and fill out surveys. The most important questions were health-related issues—how many children in the household, how many were sick, the incidence of cancer, etc.

The job was a lot of legwork, but the pay was pretty good—for a student—and the work was interesting. By the end of the summer, I didn't detect any major sicknesses caused by the accident. I told my coordinator my last week that I enjoyed the work and I hoped that it was useful. Once again, I had managed to save close to two thousand dollars, and I was looking forward to spending my last year in graduate school with Elsie.

Elsie and I found a first-floor apartment in East Oak Lane. It felt great to be living back in the neighborhood that I was most familiar with. Not only that, Max and Rick both lived in the neighborhood. I had a girlfriend and my two best friends within easy walking distance. What more could a guy ask for?

I registered for my classes and started buying my books. One more year to go! After living on a TA's salary for two years, I was anxious to start making some real money.

Elsie and I weren't sure if we were in love with each other—we just knew that we were attracted to one another. Our schedules were so busy that it seemed like all we did was sleep together. At least the sex was good.

I was studying with George Kennedy, the famous e.e. cummings scholar, and teaching three classes. I had lost my copyediting job to a graduate student in the philosophy department. I suppose that was only fair, but I did miss the extra money. Fortunately, two can live cheaper than one. The rent on our apartment was only three hundred dollars per month, which Elsie and I split. I was slowly going through the two grand I had saved during the summer, but I didn't care because I was having such a good time with Elsie. We went to the Academy of Music together, we ate out just about every other night, and she let me play with my friends whenever I felt like it. What a terrific woman!

Things were going along just swimmingly when something happened one evening that made me wonder about the safety of the neighborhood we were living in. I still hadn't given up cigarettes—I thought they helped me concentrate on my studies. I had run out, and there was a 7-11 a half block from our apartment. I had bought my cigarettes and was walking home when I sensed that something was wrong. As I looked back over my shoulder, I saw a gang of ten or eleven young blacks trying to catch up with me. Stories of these "wolfpacks" had appeared in the papers. There was brazenness in numbers, and there were reports all over town that their victims were not only mugged but also seriously hurt. I was only a hundred yards from my apartment, and I took off in a full run. I could hear some taunting from behind me, but I dared not look back or slow my pace. Once inside my apartment, I told Elsie what had happened. She was also concerned about the safety of the neighborhood, and she was glad that she was living with someone who could protect her.

This was the second near-violent experience I had since moving to the big city. I made a promise to myself that I would never go out alone at night again. I knew that I had made the right decision to high tail it and run. I felt relieved that I had prevented a possible crime. I'm not sure what would have happened if they had caught up to me, and I was glad that I didn't have to find out.

Besides the "wolfpacks," there was another source of crime in Philadelphia that outsiders had difficulty in understanding—The Philly Mob. Over the last several years, there had been a series of "hits" as various factions tried to take over the mob infrastructure. They were all Italian, of course, and their assassinations for the most part didn't affect the population at large. The "wolfpacks" were more of a menace to the general population than the mob. Their target was anyone out alone at night.

CHAPTER

5

As the fall turned into winter, Elsie and I saw less and less of each other. She was spending more and more time with her parents, and I was starting to wonder if I was headed for a dumping. Also about this time, the movie Rocky came out. The movie was a huge hit and it put Philadelphia on the national map. It was the story of a down-and-out underdog boxer who goes on to win the heavyweight championship. Up to this time, it was without a doubt the best boxing movie ever made. At one point in the movie, Rocky in his angst yells out, "Yo Adrian!" Adrian being his wife. For the next several months, it was "Yo" this and "Yo" that throughout the city. For a while, the south Philly Italian dialect spread like wildfire throughout the country. Even linguistics professors in the graduate English department laughed about it.

As I entered my last semester of graduate school, Elsie and I were spending less and less time together and I knew that something was seriously wrong with our relationship. Perhaps her parents were playing the non-Jewish card, I didn't know; all I knew was that I was spending more and more nights alone.

I needed to write my Master's thesis this semester. I chose to write it on Walker Percy, the southern doctor turned writer who I thought was one of the top five writers in the country. My thesis topic had been approved by Dr. Kennedy, and by March it was well underway. The other requirement for me to complete my Master's degree was to pass the comprehensive examination. I felt that I was ready for it and shouldn't have too much trouble with it. Both of these hurdles had to be completed by the middle of April. There was one further hurdle—proof of competency in a foreign language. I wasn't sure if I was up to this challenge or not because I hadn't taken French since I was an undergraduate.

Needless to say, during the first week of April I was busier than a worker bee. I was writing my thesis, studying for the comprehensive exam, and boning up on my French all at the same time as I was taking my last two classes and teaching three classes. Elsie's and my relationship was deteriorating, but I was too busy to care. I was operating on full brainpower and I couldn't let anything extraneous get in my way.

When the second week of April arrived, I submitted my Master's thesis to Dr. Kennedy, sat down for the three-hour comprehensive exam, and translated a passage of James Joyce's Finnegan's Wake from French to English. By the end of the week, I would know how all three turned out. For the next three days, I was on pins and needles, and I had no contact with my friends or my girlfriend.

I boarded the Broad Street subway on Friday morning with great trepidation. Soon I would know if I was going to be in school for another year or not. I reached the graduate lounge and saw that Dr. Kennedy had approved my thesis, and I had passed the comprehensive exam and the foreign language test! As soon as I completed my classes I was done and I could finally start making a decent living in the real world.

When I got home Friday evening, I called Elsie's parents' house and told her the news. She was very happy for me. She had dropped one class and wouldn't be able to finish with me. I felt a little sorry for her about that. I would be moving on to bigger and better things while she was still milling around in academe.

Two more papers to write and I would have my degree and be able to enter the working world. My friend Rick had finished the program a semester in front of me and had secured a job at a scientific publishing company by the name of the Institute for Scientific Communication, or ISC for short. All ISC did was publish the table of contents of just about every science journal known to man.

Rick told me that there was an opening in the President's small research department, and he said if I gave him a copy of my resume he would see that it got to the right people. I was so excited at the prospect of getting this job that I could barely focus on the remainder of my studies.

I only had a few classes left when I heard the news from Rick—ISC wanted to interview me! As if by fate, my interview was scheduled for the day after my last class. When I told Elsie the news, she was very happy for me and wanted to treat me to a celebratory dinner.

On the day that I submitted my last paper, I felt like I had accomplished the impossible and I called Max to see if he wanted to go out and celebrate with me. He had a rough semester too, and he felt like blowing off some steam.

As Max and I reached Jasper's, I could tell from the tone of his voice that Max was a little jealous of me. He still had at least three years to go to finish his Ph.D., and despite his part-time job, he knew that he would be poor during this time. He was happy for me, however, and hoped that I would get the job at ISC.

I told Max about my problems with Elsie. He had expected as much. He too had once had a high-class Jewish girlfriend, and in the end, he was dumped because her parents expected her to marry within the religion. Deep down I knew Elsie was gearing up to do the same thing to me. It was just a matter of when, not if.

Interview day arrived and I prepared by donning a sports jacket and tie with wool pants. I didn't own a suit, so this would have to do. I combed my hair and looked in the mirror—I thought I looked like a million bucks. I hopped on the subway and rode it all the way to City Hall. Then I had to hoof it from there to thirty-sixth and Market—an area known as University City Science Center. My destination was a three-story building whose façade looked like a giant computer processing card. I arrived just in time for my appointed interview. I was escorted to an office on the third floor just outside of the President's office. A moment later, the hiring manager appeared. Her name was Beta Moonbeam, and I could tell that she really liked me. She was an ex-hippie who went legit and had become a computer geek. After a half-hour, she offered me the job to be her assistant. The pay was ten thousand per year, and to me, that sounded like a gold mine.

CHAPTER

6

My first day on the job was one of the exciting days of my life. This was my first day at a professional job. All of the other lousy jobs that I had to take to get me to this point now seemed so pointless. I had to be a professional because I was wearing a tie. I liked the way I looked riding the subway, and for the first time in my life, I felt a kinship with the other worker bees on the train.

I reported to work precisely at 9:00 a.m. Beta showed me to my office—it was actually a work cubicle connected to hers by a common wall. My first assignment was to proofread a chapter of a biochemistry textbook that the company was producing. I tackled my assignment with gusto and was very careful to make sure that the job when completed, would be perfect. I was still diligently doing my job when somehow it was already lunch hour. How could time pass so quickly?

I walked around our joint wall to see what Beta was doing for lunch and saw that she was pulling a sleeping bag out of one of her cabinets. She said, "I sleep in this bag every day at lunchtime. Please don't disturb me during my nap time."

I was hungry, so I went down to Rick's office on the second floor to see what he did about lunch. He told me that he usually packed a lunch bag, but today he didn't so he said he'd take me to a restaurant within walking distance. The name of the place was Cavanaugh's, and it was about five blocks in the direction of center city. After we had both ordered sandwiches, Rick asked me, "So, how's your first day going?"

"Pretty good. My first assignment was to do some proofreading," I replied.

"You'll be doing a lot of that here," Rick said.

"Did you know that Beta takes a nap in a sleeping bag during lunch hour?" I asked.

"Everybody in the company knows it," Rick said with a laugh. "Have you met President Garman yet?" he asked.

"No, I haven't," I answered.

"Well, you probably will pretty soon," Rick said. "He built this company from the ground up—he's a real visionary," Rick added.

We paid our tabs and headed west on Market Street. I couldn't believe my first day was already half over. It seemed like the morning had gone by in an instant. As I walked past Beta's office towards my own, I noticed that she was already out of the bag and working. I sat down at my desk and recommenced my proofreading. I had a Dorland's medical dictionary ready to open if there was a word of biochemistry that I didn't know. That afternoon, I only had to use it two or three times. I only had two pages to go when I looked up at the clock and saw that it was already five o'clock. I decided that I had better ask Beta if she wanted my assignment completed today, or if it could wait until tomorrow.

"Oh, tomorrow's fine—I don't expect you to stay late on your first day," she said with a smile.

As I started walking towards Broad Street, I wondered if Elsie would be home so I could tell her how my first day went. It took fifteen minutes to get to the subway, a ten-minute wait, and then a half-hour on the train to the last stop where I got off, and then a five-minute walk to my apartment—one hour total commute time. Elsie wasn't home and must have been out studying somewhere.

CHAPTER

7

Tim Shea was the editorial director of the new biochemistry textbook that ISC was producing. He was a tall, mild-mannered man with glasses, and he was the antithesis of flamboyant Beta. I soon discovered that he and Beta were engaged in some kind of war, whose details would only be known in time.

Beta was my boss, and I always had to appear to be loyal to her. I liked Tim though, and I always tried to be nice to him. I supposed that they both had the ear of President Garman, which gave both of them confidence in their little turf battles. The fact that Beta had an assistant, me, and that Tim didn't, spoke for itself.

The biochemistry textbook that we were producing was actually a series of Venn diagrams that showed the interrelatedness of various fields of inquiry within the world of biochemistry. Nothing like this had previously been attempted. In essence, the whole book was actually more like a map than a scholarly treatise. It showed relatedness by counting citations throughout all the various science journals. The idea was fascinating, and I truly loved my job. I didn't think I could ever repay Rick enough for helping me to land this job.

My second day on the job, I completed my proofreading assignment and turned it into Beta by 10:00 a.m. She looked it over, saw that I did a thorough job, and said, "Good job." I was elated and asked her what she wanted me to do next. She pulled out an ATM card, told me her pin number, and told me to go to the bank and take out fifty dollars for her. This wasn't exactly what I had in mind, but I would gladly do this chore for her.

When I got back to the office and handed Beta her money and card back, I noticed that her face was flushed and she was acting disturbed.

"Are you O.K.?" I asked.

"Oh, yes, I just had an argument with Tim, she said. "He has no imagination," she added. I sympathized with her and just shook my head in agreement. "Your next assignment is to write a preface for the biochem book," Beta said.

"O.K., I'll give it my best shot," I replied. Now, this was a difficult assignment because in order to write a preface it was necessary to perfectly understand the concept behind the book. I was still a little fuzzy about several areas of the book, but I took this assignment as a sign that Beta really trusted me.

The rest of the day I sat in my office making notes about citations and Venn diagram "maps" and quadrant analyses, etc. I was perking along in my office when I heard talking emanating from Beta's office. I was curious, so I lifted up my head over the wall and saw a tall, blonde guy about my age talking to Beta. Beta saw the top of my head and motioned for me to come over. "This is Tom Garman," she said, "President Garman's son." I shook his hand and returned to my office. As I started pondering over the preface again, I realized that Beta was in good with the whole Garman family and that I should never side with Tim.

The next day, I slipped into my office quietly and proceeded to go to work on the preface. I had purchased a large coffee and was savoring it when Beta walked into my cube and announced, "Come with me, I want to show you something." I organized my papers and followed Beta into her office. I sat down in the chair next to her desk. On her desk was a large glass jar with holes punched in the lid and a three-foot snake in it. She held it up and asked, "How do you like Tim's present?" Her red hair twirled in the air as she quickly grabbed the jar and gave it to me.

"Is this a garner snake?" I asked.

"Yes. I want you to put it on Tim's desk," she said. "He's a snake, and this is what he deserves," she added.

I played along. "I assume you want this to be an anonymous present?" I asked.

"Of course," she said. "Even though he won't have any trouble guessing who it's from," she said with a laugh.

I grabbed the jar from the bottom and carried it back to my cube. Tim sat at his desk most of the day, and I'd have to get lucky during a bathroom break or wait until lunchtime. Tim's cube was right across the hall from Beta's, and my office had a direct view to the top of his cubicle walls.

At around 10:30 Tim got up and left his office. I seized the moment, grabbed the jar, and quickly put it on his desk. I couldn't believe what I was doing, but it was a direct order from my boss.

A few minutes later I saw Tim walking up the hall towards his office. I buried my head in my papers. "Jesus Christ!" I heard Tim yell, then a thumping footsteps towards Beta's office. "Are you crazy?" mild-mannered Tim asked Beta, with the jar in his hands. Laughing hysterically, Beta said, "I didn't put that in your office."

Tim wheeled around and put the snake jar on top of the President's secretary's desk. I remained still throughout the entire confrontation. I didn't dare move from my office.

CHAPTER

One day at lunch Rick explained to me Beta's history with President Garman. A few years ago, they had an affair. When it ended, they remained friends, and Jerry Garman put Beta in charge of his pet research projects. Now it was rumored that Beta had moved on to Jerry's son, Tom. They had been seen together going upstairs to the fourth-floor stockroom, and when they came down they would both be flushed. Not that it was anybody's business, but Beta was ten years older than Tom.

I told Rick what I had witnessed a few days ago and he just smiled at me. I also told Rick about the snake incident, and he said that wasn't the first time Beta went a little overboard. I began to fear that my boss might not be mentally stable. Not that was vitally important, as this was only my first job out of graduate school, and I was gaining valuable experience no matter what the mental status of my boss.

Rick advised me that if I wanted to keep my job, I'd better always side with Beta. Although I liked Tim Shea, I could never agree with him if he went against Beta. I learned that rule number one in the business world is self-preservation always comes first. I liked my five hundred a month paycheck and I wanted to keep it.

Rick was happily married and he and his wife were expecting their first baby. He knew that Elsie and me were almost over, and he was quite sympathetic. He liked Elsie, but he also knew how hard Jewish girls were to please.

Beta was also becoming increasingly difficult to please. Besides fetching her money and sharpening her pencils, I was now also being told how to dress. It was summer, and one day I wore shorts to work because I wanted to go jogging after work. When Beta looked at my bare legs she said, "You should wear shorts more often." I wasn't sure if she was serious or not, but I secretly liked the compliment.

According to Beta, Tim was a very conscientious editor who just couldn't see "the big picture." He had evidently been chastised by President Garman because he was no longer defiant but compliant. He kept to himself and did his work and spoke with nothing but humility in his voice. It was working—Beta was starting to like him again.

It was August 1980, and I had finally received my diploma in the mail. When I received it I told Elsie, and she said she wanted to take me out to dinner to celebrate. I wasn't stupid, and I knew that this was probably going to be my dumping dinner.

When I got home from work that day, Elsie was home and she was dressed to the ts. She had on a bright red blouse, black skirt, and heels, and I knew that I was dead. We went to an Italian restaurant in Jenkintown. We both ordered linguini with clam sauce and two glasses of Chianti. She really looked beautiful, and I was practically drooling onto my plate. She waited until the dinner was almost over.

"I love you, but it's time for me to move on," she said. "Move where?" I asked.

"I'm moving back in with my parents. You can have the apartment. I still have several years of schooling left and you're already out in the working world. We're not in the same place anymore," she said.

I knew it was coming and I couldn't even pretend to be surprised. "Was it my friends?" I asked.

"No, your friends are fine," she said.

"What if I go back to school with you?" I asked. "My boss is crazy and I'd give up my job in a minute to be with you," I said.

"Don't lie to me," she said. "You love your job and your crazy boss."

Why do women have to be so damned smart? "O.K. If that's what you want. I'll always love you," I said.

She finally didn't have an answer for that one. We paid the bill and went back to the apartment. She let me have her one more time, and it was bittersweet. God, Jewish girls are good in bed! She left sometime in the middle of the night, and I awoke long enough to know that I would be alone in the morning.

CHAPTER

Now that I was living alone again, I had to pay for the three hundred dollars a month apartment by myself. That left me with only two hundred dollars a month spending money, and that was with having a full-time job. I soon realized that I wasn't that much better off than when I was a TA. That really rattled me. Not only that, Beta was starting to treat me more and more like her personal assistant instead of her research assistant. Besides fetching her money, sharpening her pencils, and "gopher" this and "gopher" that, she was also starting to make sexual innuendos. She had a lascivious smile on her face every time I wore shorts to work. I didn't dare tell her that I had just broken up with my girlfriend, or I'm sure the sexual harassment would get worse.

One day while I was sitting quietly in my office, I heard a commotion coming from Tim's office. As I peeked over the top of my office walls, I noticed two armed security guards standing there and one of them said, "Come with us please, and bring your badge." I knew that Tim's number was up. I let my glance move over to Beta's office and I just got a glimpse of her beaming from ear to ear. I finally decided that she was evil and that I was going to start looking for a new job.

I started looking in the newspapers for a new job because I knew that my tenure at ISC would be short-lived. I also started "networking," the new term for asking all your friends if they knew of any openings.

Finally, one day at lunch, Rick mentioned that he had heard of an editor named Bernie Grayburn who worked for a pharmaceutical company and was looking for a science writer. As soon as he mentioned this, I was intrigued. I knew that between my education and my experience as a research assistant that I had the credentials for the job. I asked him where the job was located and he said, "Out in the western suburbs."

I had never been to the western suburbs of Philadelphia and I wondered what it was like. I got Grayburn's address from Rick and sent him a copy of my resume. In the meantime, I kept a low profile and bided my time.

I suppose it was inevitable that with the prospects of a new job that I would run into trouble with Beta. I told her that I wouldn't fetch her money anymore and to start treating me like a research assistant instead of her personal slave. I knew at that point that I was destined for the same fate as Tim if I didn't get the science-writing job at the pharmaceutical company. I couldn't help it that at just the prospect of that job that I was bolder and cockier. I knew that Beta was quietly lining up her ducks because after every conversation she would take a few minutes to document everything said. Good for her, I thought to myself, because I'll be out of here before she gets to her final duck.

About a week after I had sent in my resume, I finally heard back. I had gotten an interview with Grayburn! I was walking on clouds the whole next day. I was as sweet as I could be to Beta, and I knew she was wondering what the hell was going on. Let her guess, I thought to myself, for soon I would be earning pharmaceutical wages instead of publishing wages. I could taste the glory; soon I would no longer be poor.

I took a personal day the day of my interview. I wanted to be able to totally focus on my interview and not have anything else on my mind. I still didn't own a suit, so I decided to go for the academic look—Harris Tweed jacket with charcoal gray wool pants and a blue tie.

In the morning I had polished my shoes so that they shone. I looked in the mirror—geeze I was good-looking. What boss in their right mind would turn down this handsome dude, I thought to myself.

My itinerary called for riding the subway to City Hall, then taking Amtrak to a town named Radnor. The company was only a block from the Radnor train station. I was so excited that I almost forgot my briefcase as I was walking out the door in the morning. That would have been a disaster because I had all my writing samples stuffed into my briefcase. Halfway out the door, I noticed it sitting next to the dining room table. I grabbed it and headed out the door.

On the subway, there was the usual mixture of black and white, young and old, haggard and well dressed. I got off at the City Hall stop and headed for Amtrak. I got on and walked to the back of my car and sat down.

I immediately noticed a difference between the people on the subway and those on this train. Here, nobody was poorly dressed. Everyone sort of looked "preppy," and almost all the men were wearing suits. I was well dressed enough not to feel conspicuous. I also noticed that the women almost invariably had expensive-looking jewelry and very nice clothes.

I got off the train at Radnor and headed for the entrance to Wyatt Pharmaceuticals, which was visible from the train stop. After walking through the doors, I approached the receptionist and told her that I had an appointment with Bernie Grayburn at eleven o'clock. She dialed his extension and she said, He'll be here shortly." I sat down in the waiting area and tried to collect my wits.

A short, dark-haired man walked through the revolving door and I knew it was Grayburn immediately. "Hi, I'm Bernie Grayburn," he said. I followed him back to his office and took a seat. As I showed him my writing samples, I could tell he was impressed. He particularly liked the chapter that I had written on beta-adrenergic receptors. He explained that his company was working on a drug in this area to treat heart disease. I knew that this was a big plus in my favor, but I didn't want to seem overconfident.

He told me that all documents were written in a word-processing software program called WordPerfect. With this program, it was easy to make changes and the whole process was speeded up by ten-fold. This new technology had only been implemented within the past year or so, and Grayburn had been instrumental in setting up the current system.

I left his office fairly confident of getting the job. What an improvement in my lifestyle there would be if I got this job. The people on this side of town were so much more—refined—than the people I was used to. I wanted this job.

CHAPTER

The next few days I was on pins and needles waiting to hear if I had gotten the science writing job or not. Things were deteriorating rapidly with Beta and ISC, and all I had was hope that I would be delivered and saved from my current circumstances. I found out through Rick that the area of town that I had visited for my interview was called the "Main Line." It got its name from the railroad that ran westward out of the city. Rick told me that the Main Line was where the richest people in Philadelphia live. Now it all made sense—the nice clothes, the preppy outfits, the jewelry. This was the rich part of town, and this is where I would have to move if I got the new job.

In the meantime, Beta was becoming more like Medusa with each passing day. My assignments were increasingly criticized, and I knew that she knew that something was up. With Tim gone, she needed a new enemy, and now that target was on my head. She had put me on probation for "insubordination." I was rather proud of that and bragged about it to Rick. He was concerned about me, but I told him that I thought the interview had gone well and that I thought that I was going to get the job.

Beta was still a duck or two short and was running around like a banshee gathering support. I was now a persona non grata within the research department, and yet I couldn't hide my optimism. I was secretly praying that Grayburn would call me with good news. I had a meeting with Beta at four o'clock in the afternoon, and I wondered if that was the end. At around two o'clock my phone rang. I answered it and said, "Hello."

"Hello, this is Bernie Grayburn. I'm offering you the job," he said.

"That's great!" I said. "Thank you so much." "When can you start?" Grayburn asked.

"I'll give two weeks' notice today," I said. "I guess that means I can start on the fifteenth," I added.

"Very well, I'll see you then, and congratulations," Grayburn said.

"Thanks again, Bernie," I said. "I won't disappoint you."

I had a secret sense of satisfaction within me because now, no matter what happened, I was going into my four o'clock meeting well-armed. I overheard Beta exhale with giddy laughter, and I interpreted that to mean that she may have lined up her last duck, but it no longer mattered. I was now one of the elects, a science writer in the pharmaceutical industry, and even if I survived the four o'clock meeting, I would be tendering my resignation immediately afterward.

As the minute hand on the clock ticked away, I actually began to feel sorry for Beta. She was so eccentric that she would never be hired for the job that I was about to take, and I was starting to feel grateful towards her. If she hadn't hired me, I wouldn't have gotten the experience that I needed to get the pharmaceutical job, so I decided that whatever happened at four o'clock, I would be polite and humble.

I headed for Beta's office at four o'clock and when she said we needed to go downstairs to Personnel, I knew it was over. I was poised and calm and she didn't like it. We reached an office with an HR person waiting for us and we both sat down.

The HR woman said, "You are not performing up to expectations, and you are being terminated. Please give me your badge." I took my badge off my belt and handed it to her.

"I just want to thank you for the experience I got working here," I said looking at Beta. "I wish you good luck in completing the book." With that, I turned on my heels and walked out of the office, out of the building, and down the street. I had two weeks to kick around and do whatever I wanted and I felt as free as a bird.

I cashed my last check from ISC and realized that I would have to be frugal in order to get through the two weeks before I started my new job. I would also have to start looking for a new apartment on the Main Line.

I called Max and told him about the new job, and he was very happy for me. I asked him if he wanted to go out and celebrate with me, and he said he did. We went to Jasper's because it could be the last time. I ordered two beers and handed one to Max.

"You did good," Max said as he raised his glass in salute.

"Thanks, I know," I said.

Max was still in graduate school and living on a student budget, and here I was about to make the big bucks in the pharmaceutical industry. I was even four years younger than Max. That had to hurt. I treated Max to another round.

"You know, I have to find an apartment out on the Main Line," I said to Max.

"Yep, I guess you do," he replied. "I hope I can afford one," I said. "You'll find something," he said.

I knew he was right. I was young and clean-cut, and I knew that I could find something to fit my budget. I decided that tomorrow that would be my goal.

The next day I explored the Main Line. The houses were big, but not all of them, and I felt that I would be able to find a reasonably priced apartment. I stumbled across Valley Forge Park, where General Washington spent the winter of 1777-78. The park was only a few miles off the Main Line. There was a new tall apartment building just off the park, and I decided to give it a try. There was a vacancy on the fifteenth floor, and after looking it over, I put down a security deposit. I would be able to move in the following week.

I called Max and told him that I had found an apartment near Valley Forge Park. I invited him to go visit the place with me, but he decided that he was just too busy.

I started organizing my stuff for the move at my East Oak Lane apartment. I let myself revel in nostalgia as I thought about me and Elsie. If only this, if only that we would have been happy, I thought to myself. Some of the furniture didn't even belong to me—they were Elsie's. They belonged to me now by the law of eminent domain. Dave and Rick both said they would help me move, so I'd have to have some beer on hand. After all, it was a universal standard that every moving party gets rewarded with beer.

The day of the move, I rented a small U-Haul van. That was all I really needed because everything I had was really small. Towards the end of the move, Rick had some news for me. Even Beta was in trouble at ISC. Evidently, somehow president Garman found out that Beta was having an affair with his son, and he was very upset about it. He said that if I thought she was bad before, I should see her now. I told Rick that I was glad that I was moving on to better things.

Everything I had fit into the thousand-square-foot apartment fifteen stories above the earth. From my balcony, I could see almost all of Valley Forge Park, and the view was spectacular. I liked being perched this high above the ground. My nest was much higher than most birds.

CHAPTER

I used the next few days before starting my new job to set up my apartment and put everything in its place. I started in the kitchen, putting all my pots and pans away, and the silverware and dinnerware. Next, I tackled the living room, setting up my sofa and TV. Lastly, I set up my bed in the bedroom and put all my clothes away in the beautiful walk-in closet.

In all, it took three days to get everything in its place. When I was finished, I looked at each room with satisfaction. Without a doubt, this was the nicest place I had ever lived, excluding my childhood home. I looked out over Valley Forge Park, and everything was green for as far as the eye could see, and I truly felt at home. In three days I would be starting my new job as a science writer, and I felt like I really deserved to live in a place as nice as this.

I could sense that Max was a little jealous. He saw what the prospect of a good job could buy you, and he knew that he had to wait at least three more years before he could afford a place as nice as this. I made it clear to him that he was welcome to come over any time he felt like it, and we could scope out girls in the park together.

I was becoming very excited in anticipation of starting my new job. I wanted to become the best science writer in the world. I would let no detail escape me, and I would do well and get raises every year and move out of the middle class and into the upper middle class. Such were my dreams.

After paying my security deposit and one month's rent, I only had enough money left to purchase one article of clothing before starting my new job. I decided on a new tie. I only had a few of them, and none of them looked outright dapper. I drove to the King of Prussia Mall and went straight to Brooks Brothers. I picked up an all-silk tie and took it to the cashier. It cost forty-two dollars. I was horrified at the price, but I paid it and quickly left. Tomorrow I was entering a new world, and I wanted to look as good as possible.

That night I had many dreams. I dreamed of my first paycheck. I dreamed of buying designer suits and cashmere sweaters. I dreamed of buying a really nice car and taking really hot women on dates in it.

My dreams ended at seven a.m. when I awoke and realized I had to get through my first day as a science writer in the pharmaceutical industry. I showered and shaved, went to the bathroom, and got dressed. The finishing touch was my new silk blue tie from Brooks Brothers.

I jumped into my VW beetle and headed for the Wyatt Laboratories parking lot. I got to the receptionist's desk, and she buzzed me through the glass doors. I reached Grayburn's office on the third floor and waved at him from the hallway. He was on the phone, but he looked up at me and smiled. He motioned me to come in and sit down.

When he got off the phone, he said, "Welcome to Wyatt Laboratories."

"Good to be here," I replied.

"I'm going to assign you to the rheumatoid arthritis team," Grayburn said. "You will be reporting to Dr. Harrison," he added. "Let me show you to your office," he said as he got up and headed for the door. I followed him down the hall until he came to a twelve by twelve-foot office with a computer sitting on the desk.

"Here it is," Grayburn said. "It's very nice," I said.

"Go through the desk and cabinets and make sure you have everything you need," Grayburn said. "At twelve o'clock, stop by my office and I'll take you out to lunch."

I was already playing with the computer and checking out the desk. I thought I'd give myself an hour before reporting to Dr. Harrison. The hour went by in a flash, and I found Dr. Harrison sitting at his desk.

"Welcome," he said. "I've written all the instructions down for your first assignment. If you have any questions, please come see me."

"Thank you, Dr. Harrison, I will," I replied.

I took my assignment back to my desk and started to read it. I can do this, I said to myself.

I spent the rest of my first day reading over my first assignment and thinking about my new wages. I had doubled my ISC salary, and my new take-home pay would be about a thousand a month, a veritable fortune. I sat there at my desk staring down at my blue silk tie and thinking about how lucky I had been.

Finally, after seven years of college and numerous "grunge" jobs, I had finally arrived. Science writing for a pharmaceutical company was an upper-middle-class job. My parents were definitely only middle-class people, and I had moved a notch up the social ladder and I was proud of it.

When five o'clock came, I stuffed my work into a leather attaché case and actually intended to work on it at home. I wanted my first assignment to be perfect, and if that meant doing a little extra work at home, so be it.

I found my car in the enormous parking lot, hopped in, and headed back towards Valley Forge. I arrived home and got on the elevator to the fifteenth floor. Once inside my apartment, I walked out into my balcony to survey the sereneness of Valley Forge Park. I was twenty-six years old and I felt like I was on top of the world.

CHAPTER

I called Max to see if he wanted to go out. To my surprise, he said he did. I drove the half-hour to East Oak Lane and took the elevator to his second-floor apartment. There was another friend of Max's there—Dave— who was going to go out with us. He was another graduate sociology student and a musician. It turned out that Dave was having girlfriend trouble and Max invited him over to console him.

Dave's girlfriend, Jane, had taken a beach vacation with a group of girlfriends, and when she came back she confessed that she had cheated on him. Dave, of course, was devastated, and now they were on the verge of splitting up.

I told Dave about Elsie splitting up with me over education issues, but that didn't seem to cheer him up. Both Max and I said that anybody who would do that to him didn't deserve him. That sentiment did seem to cheer him up, and then we started to enjoy ourselves.

We scoped out the room, and there were two pretty blondes sitting in the corner. Max said he knew one of them from a party, and he went over and started talking with them. After a few minutes, he motioned for Dave and me to come over.

The blondes were named Debbie and Susan, and Max had met them at a party. Max introduced Dave and me, and then he excused himself to go to the bathroom. The conversation died as soon as Max left, and then Dave said, "I'm in the process of breaking up with my girlfriend—she cheated on me while she was on vacation."

With that, the girls opened up again and started commiserating with Dave. A few minutes later, we had their phone numbers. That's what I loved about Max—he always knew how to break the ice, and his friends always benefited from that.

Back at work the next day, I felt a little guilty that I hadn't finished my work assignment at home. I saw the coffee cart coming around the corner and I made a mad dash for it. I bought a sixteen-ounce cup of strong coffee and took it back to my desk. I lit up a cigarette. I figured between the caffeine and the nicotine that I had to be as wide awake as I would ever get. I tackled my assignment with gusto.

By eleven thirty, I took my work and handed it in to Dr. Harrison. He gave me a new assignment, and it was much more complicated than my first assignment. I thanked him and walked back to my office. I was thinking about Dave and how it must feel to have a significant other cheats on you. I couldn't think of anything worse.

Bernie Grayburn and I were fast becoming friends. I would visit him in his office, and he would regale me with stories of his experiences in the military in Turkey and Afghanistan. I tried to show my appreciation for giving me the job by listening with keen interest. Bernie had received word from Dr. Harrison that my first assignment had been a success.

We went out to lunch together, and he ordered a beer to go with his lunch. I ordered one too just to be sociable. "Dr. Harrison is very ambitious," Grayburn said. "I know that he wants my job," he added.

"Really," I replied. "He doesn't seem like a backstabber to me," I added.

"Well, you're just getting to know him," Grayburn said. "You'll see him a little more clearly after a few weeks," he added.

With that, we paid our tab and left the restaurant. Grayburn put a Bob Marley tape on his car stereo and said, "You've got to go with the flow, move with the groove, and everything will be alright."

I wasn't sure exactly what he meant by that, but I was slightly buzzed and figured it would sink in later. At least for the rest of that day, it never did.

My focus in life became grinding out clinical study reports like there was no tomorrow. Dr. Harrison was pleased with how quickly I adapted to the job. Having moved to the East Coast from the West, I knew that my future was in pharmaceuticals.

After a few weeks on the job, I got a feel for the rhythm of the work. The average clinical study report took two weeks to write. It was a laborious job, but it was a prestigious job and the pay was excellent. I liked the detail required to do the job, and I was very careful to cross each t and dot each i. Grayburn was happy with my progress, and the reports back to him from Dr. Harrison were favorable. And the best part—I was living just off the Main Line! No more wolf packs, no more Broad Street subway. The people out here all wore preppy clothes and drove fancy cars, and had fancy jobs. Here, I was in the majority, not the minority.

When I got home from work, I kicked off my shoes and walked around in my socks over the plush carpeting. I started making huge vats of chili that would last for a week so that I would have extra time to go play in Valley Forge Park after work.

Thus, I continued to work hard and play hard. I thought that play was just as important as work, and my lifestyle reflected that. I made sure that I was always at least five minutes early to work, and that was a wise strategy because precisely at nine o'clock in the morning, Dr. Harrison conducted a "bed check" to make sure that all employees working for him were on time. There was never a bed check in the evening, only in the morning, so leaving a few minutes before five o'clock was no big deal.

I was a keen observer and a quick study, and I learned early on how to play the game.

I continued to go out with Max whenever his schedule allowed. I could tell that Max was happy for me, but I knew that he would be a big success someday too. We went to a place called The Greenhouse, a bar on the Main Line. We ordered a couple of beers, and who walks over was none other than Jane, Dave's ex-girlfriend. She was more of a go-getter than I originally thought. She was getting her Master's degree in physical therapy at Penn, and she was impressed with me being a science writer in the pharmaceutical industry. Max was a little disappointed, but I asked her for her phone number.

In my own defense, I had no idea how attracted I would be to Jane. What she had done to Dave was morally reprehensible, but I couldn't help myself. She was hot and I hadn't been laid in months.

I decided to do the right thing and ask Max to ask Dave if it was O.K. with him if I asked her out. Max was uncomfortable with the request, but he said he would do it.

After a few days, he got back to me and told me that Dave was O.K. with it. I thought about calling Dave myself, but I chickened out and decided against it. Instead, I called Jane and she was happy to hear from me. I asked her out and she said yes. Evidently, she was attracted to me too.

CHAPTER

I was getting good reviews at work, and I thought that the prospect of having a woman again in my life was helping me in this regard. There was a new edge to my self-confidence, something just perceptible beneath the surface.

In addition to always arriving five minutes early to work, I also turned in all my assignments a day or two early. After a few weeks of this, I gained a reputation as a fast, reliable worker.

My first date with Jane, we went to go see a new band named Only Human. We had a great time together, and we both knew that there was mutual chemistry. After our first date, I knew it was only a matter of time before we slept together. That buoyed my spirits at work as well as at home, and it was also giving me a little bit of machismo.

For our second date, I invited Jane over to my apartment for dinner. I was preparing chicken with mushrooms. I arrived home at five o'clock from work and quickly proceeded to start cooking dinner. The key to the success of the dinner was the secret ingredient that went into the mushroom sauce—vermouth! A shot of vermouth gave the mushroom sauce that extra zing that it needed.

Jane arrived at my door promptly at six, and I told her to sit down while I poured her a glass of wine. She obeyed me and said, "Thank you." I served the dinner and sat down and started to eat. I asked her, "Well, what do you think?"

"It's delicious," she said.

"How do you like the sauce?" I asked. "What's in it, it's wonderful," she said. "There's a hint of vermouth in it," I said. "No wonder I like it!" she exclaimed.

We finished the meal, and I dug some ice cream out of the freezer. As I set it down on the table, I said, "Hey—why don't I call Max and see what he's doing? Maybe he'll want to go out with us."

At that, Jane got excited and said, "That's a great idea!"

I called Max, and as I started talking to him something very strange happened. Jane started licking her lips in a lascivious way and I knew what she was thinking. I was starting to get an erection and she could see me growing. She got up from the table and got on her knees in front of me. I unzipped my trousers and opened up my underpants for my penis to spring out. Perhaps she wanted to see if I could keep my cool as I was getting a blowjob while talking to my best friend on the phone. I didn't know, but she was sucking me off like there was no tomorrow.

The amazing thing is that I kept my concentration and didn't lose the thread of the conversation with Max. But, on the other hand, no matter how bad I wanted to, I couldn't cum while I was still talking to him. That was the mental block. Calmly, I said, "Bye Max," and I grabbed Jane and escorted her into my bedroom. I was finally able to climax during intercourse with her.

Back at work, for the first time, I allowed myself a little time for rumination. After dwelling on it for a while, I realized that just the sound of Max's voice over the phone is what had made Jane so horny. She really wanted max, and I was just a pawn in her love life chess game. Given her history, this should not have been so surprising to me.

Grayburn was on to me that there was a woman in my life, but he was too clever to say anything. Dr. Harrison noted that I was a little cockier than before, but as long as I did good work he didn't care. I pleased him by being a detail-oriented grunt, even though I didn't suck up to him quite as much as when I started.

My first paycheck made me feel wealthy. All those years in graduate school had paid off, and I finally felt like I was making what I was worth. The money also had the same effect as the testosterone running through my veins—it made me horny. I had never thought about the correlation between sex drive and money before; I was navigating uncharted territory. All I knew is that I wanted to bang Jane to kingdom come and enjoy every minute of it.

After another day of work, on the drive home to Valley Forge, a great idea occurred to me. Maine was beautiful in August: why not ask Jane to take a vacation with me to Maine to visit my Uncle Robert before the season was over? I'd bang her every night while on vacation, but I would be the proper, respectable boyfriend when we visited her parents in Torrington, Connecticut.

I had been at Wyatt Laboratories just long enough to take a week's vacation. When I got home, I dialed her number and asked her if she would do it. She said yes without hesitation.

The plans were made and I called Uncle Robert to tell him that we were coming. He was very excited about it and looked forward to our visit. I got out of work at five o'clock and drove home to get my suitcase. Jane lived in Roxborough, so I had to navigate the Schuylkill Expressway to pick her up.

When I got there, she was still ditsying around; she wasn't the most organized woman in the world.

"Do you need help?" I asked.

"Just give me fifteen minutes and I'll be ready," she replied.

She finally got everything together and I carried her three suitcases to the car. We finally jumped in the car and headed north. We were driving straight through to

Camden, Maine where we had reservations at a bed and breakfast.

Uncle Robert was recently divorced, and he couldn't accommodate us right now. That was just as well because I planned on having sex with Jane every night, and I didn't want to embarrass her.

We arrived in Camden at three a.m. fortunately, there was an emergency buzzer for late arrivals. We buzzed it, and in five minutes the owner greeted us in a robe and gave us our room key. I thanked her, and we went to our room. It was rustic but nice, and after getting our suitcases in, we fell asleep within fifteen minutes.

CHAPTER

S aturday morning rose bright and beautiful in Maine, and Jane and I didn't get out of bed until eleven a.m. We headed for the main office building for breakfast. It was only a continental breakfast, but the coffee tasted wonderful and we were both able to fill up on Danishes. After eating, we hopped into the car and headed for Camden.

There was a small marina in Camden, and we stopped to admire its beauty. A bar's back deck turned into a wharf on the marina, and as we walked into the bar, we saw that this was the week of the Camden Jazz Festival. We knew that we were in for some good music.

We found Uncle Robert's farmhouse off some back country road and pulled up to the house. He came out to greet us.

"This is my girlfriend Jane. How you doing Uncle Robert?" I said.

"Nice to meet you Jane," Uncle Robert said as he gave me a hug. "Come on in."

The farmhouse was rustic but clean as a whistle, with beautiful furniture spread throughout the house.

"I didn't know we came the week of the Camden Jazz Festival," I said. "What a bonus!"

"Oh, yes," Uncle Robert said. "I'm sure you'll hear some great music."

After the tour of the house, Uncle Robert took us outside to show us his land. He had bought twenty-six acres of Maine virgin forest, and only four or five acres had been cleared; the rest was still unspoiled forest. After walking down the trail, Jane and I were nearly mesmerized by the forest's beauty.

I don't know what made me broach the subject, but I asked Uncle Robert, "How is Aunt Kate doing?"

"She's fine," Uncle Robert replied with a hint of sadness in his voice. "We were happy together for twenty years," he added.

"My parents really liked Aunt Kate," I couldn't help from blurting out.

We came across an ancient pick-up truck parked deep in the woods, and Uncle Robert told us to hop in. The muffler sputtered a few times and then the engine sounded smooth and we headed back to the farmhouse.

I could tell that Jane was very impressed with Uncle Robert, and that made me happy. Uncle Robert was an aristocrat who was bound to impress any woman. It dawned on me that maybe this was the whole point of this vacation—to impress Jane so that she would keep wanting to go to bed with me. I knew there was an element of truth in this thought, but I tucked it away for future reference.

After saying goodbye to Uncle Robert, we headed back to Camden for dinner. We both ordered lobster and we stuffed ourselves on lobster and beer until Herbie Mann's Orchestra played jazz all night and we both got quite drunk, but not drunk enough to not have sex when we got back to our cabin.

In the morning, we headed south for Torrington, Connecticut. When we arrived, I was given a third-floor garret for a bedroom, and Jane told me that she would make up for it when we got home. I was on my best behavior, of course, and I tried to be as polite as possible. Jane was one of fourteen children, and there was always a commotion going on somewhere in the house.

After breakfast, we headed out to explore the Berkshire Mountains in northwest Connecticut. Jane was a nature lover like I was, and we climbed the hills like little children exploring the world.

We spent all day hiking the mountains, coming down only at dinnertime. We drove into town and pulled into the first restaurant we found. We gorged ourselves and had plenty to drink before heading back to Jane's parents' house. We kissed goodnight and I went up to my garret bedroom and went to bed. We would be back in Philadelphia tomorrow; our little getaway would be over.

In the morning, I awoke and went downstairs to see if Jane was awake yet. She was already up and making breakfast for the two of us. Afterward, we loaded our suitcases into the car, and then headed west to New York and then south to Philadelphia.

I dropped her off at her apartment and told her I wanted to rest up before going back to work. I was tired, but I had the time of my life.

CHAPTER

The next day, even though my exhaustion, I was eager to get back to work. It was my job that gave me the money to live this way, and I wanted to do well at any cost.

Bernie asked me how my vacation went, and I told him it went great. While I was away, Dr. Harrison had three more staff members reporting to him. He now had more people reporting to him than Bernie. There was nothing Bernie could do about it; Dr. Harrison had the creds to be a big shot, and in this business, that's what it's all about. At least Bernie knew where he stood.

So far at least, Dr. Harrison hadn't asked me to do anything to undermine Bernie's position, and I was grateful for that. At least Dr. Harrison was playing fair.

Slowly but surely, I was making a reputation for myself as the consummate good employee—early to work, diligent at work, and always prepared to help out. With my new income, I could well afford my nest above Valley Forge Park, and soon I would be able to afford a new car.

Success on the job became my number one priority. I double-checked and triple-checked my work before handing it in, and I was always on time.

I know that one of the things that attracted Jane to me was my job as a science writer. In this occupation, you have to be serious-minded to do well, and Jane saw that trait in me. On the opposite side, I knew Jane had to be smart as hell just to get into Penn.

One day, I was given an assignment where I could really shine if I did a good job. The assignment was to write a brochure describing all the pharmaceutical products in the company's pipeline. This job entailed collaboration with a medical illustrator, but I would be known throughout the company if it was a success.

I realized that I was not a man without ambition. Here was my chance to be a star within the department. I had gotten the job, gotten a girl, and now I was in the process of getting the feather in my cap.

After a few weeks of work, I knew that I had a gem of a brochure on my hands. Mark, the medical illustrator, had made my text come alive in living color. When I showed it to Bernie he said, "This is beautiful." He showed it to Paul "Useless" Uzbek, the head of clinical operations. After it came back from the printers, it was distributed throughout the department, and I was the new "it" guy in the department.

My head reeling with success, I called Jane and asked her if she wanted to celebrate with me at the London Victory Club. I had gone there several times with Max to chase women, and during its prime was known as the premier party destination in the city. She gave me her congratulations and said yes she wanted to go.

After work, I picked her up and we headed for center city. The London Victory Club was on Chestnut between Eighth and Ninth streets. I found a lucky parking spot on Seventh, and we walked the block to the club.

Inside, music videos were playing on wide-screen TVs, and people were dancing. I bought a couple of martinis and handed one to Jane. I asked her to dance and we started grinding to the music.

During the second song, I noticed that Jane was distracted. When I followed her gaze, I saw that she was looking at another friend of Max's, Joey. I had met him once or twice before at parties, but I didn't really know him that well. His moniker was Joey The Urban Tracker. I don't know how he got that nickname, but everyone called him that. I could tell that Jane wanted to meet him, so I said, "Let's go talk to Joey."

I introduced them, and I could see that Jane was impressed with him, but Jane was my girlfriend now, and damnit, Joey shouldn't have looked so interested. We talked about the parties where we had met and I asked him where he was living.

"Oh, I rent a row house in Fairmount," Joey replied. "It's convenient to center city but a lot quieter there," he added.

I told him that I was living near Valley Forge and that I worked on the Main Line.

"Oh, the Main Line, with the rich people," Joey said with a laugh.

"Well, not everybody's rich, but there are a lot of them," I replied. The next thing I knew, Jane grabbed Joey's arm and dragged him out on the dance floor with her. They gyrated together for a few tunes, and when they got back, Jane said, "We'd better go—I have work tomorrow."

I drove her back to her apartment, and she invited me in. "Let's take a bath together," she said. Jane had nice tits, and once in the tub I immediately got an erection.

She started stroking me and I was in heaven. With towels on, we got up from the tub and walked to her bedroom, where Jane put her hands on her chest of drawers and spread her legs. I did her doggie-style standing up until I came deep in her pussy. There was something about Jane and other men that really turned her on.

CHAPTER

The success of my brochure was still reverberating around the walls and halls of Wyatt Laboratories. Bernie touted my talent to all the important physicians in Clinical Research, and my stock was definitely on the rise. I sensed that there was something fair in the wind as I continued to please Dr. Harrison.

By the end of the week, my hunch was confirmed. On Friday morning, Dr. Harrison walked into my office and told me that he was promoting me from junior medical writer to full medical writer, with a full ten percent increase in salary. I wanted to hug him, but instead, I just said "Thank you."

Evidently, the brochure had put me over the top. I called Max and told him the good news, and he said that was worthy of a celebration. I told him that I would meet him at Jasper's at seven o'clock.

At Jasper's, we started off by my telling Max that I wasn't happy about how Jane had acted in front of The Urban Tracker. Max told me not to trust him, and that he may try to steal Jane from me. I got a little upset by this and told him that I had never been ditched for another man before. He told me that was in women's nature and to get used to it.

I wasn't going to let this news spoil my promotion celebration, so I started drinking more. I sucked down two martinis and then ordered a kamikaze. Max was still a student, so he kept right up with me.

I looked around the room, and there were a number of attractive women sitting in groups of two or three, and I realized that even though I had a girlfriend, I was still attracted to them and wanted to make a move on them. Suddenly, it dawned on me that maybe I was no better than Jane. I realized that if I did lose Jane to The Urban Tracker, I had to be a man about it. I had to remember the good times and then move on.

Even though I was able to focus at work, I couldn't get Joey The Urban Tracker off my mind. I had visions of Jane leaving me for him, and despite this, I couldn't find a way to dislike him. If it happened, I knew it would be at Jane's instigation, not his.

When I received my first paycheck with my new pay raise in it, I was able to shuck my thoughts about Joey and feel like I was still on top of the world. Even Dr. Harrison had to be careful while I was basking in my glory because he knew my brochure had pleased the top brass.

The more I thought about my current circumstances the happier I became. I was no longer the bottom man on the totem pole, and I had really staged a coup with the brochure. I wasn't about to let a <u>possible</u> love rival ruin my life.

It was September, and most of the crowds at the shore would be gone. I decided to ask Jane to go to the shore with me for the weekend. She said yes, so I called a hotel named The Mad Hatter and booked a room.

I picked her up Friday after work and drove the three hours to Cape May, New Jersey. After checking into our hotel, we went looking for a good restaurant. I treated her to dinner and then we went for a walk along the beach. The ocean water was still seventy-two degrees even though there was a little chill in the mid-September air.

Out of nowhere, I said, "You know, what you did to Dave was really wrong." I couldn't believe I had said it, but there it was out in the open. I could see that she was hurt.

"I know it was wrong, but what does that have to do with us?" she asked.

"Everything," I replied.

CHAPTER

17

Back at work, after I thought about it, I realized that what I had said to Jane was probably the harshest thing I had ever said to anybody in my life. I still couldn't believe I said it, and I wondered how much longer we'd be a couple.

Ironically, things couldn't be doing any better at work. The crest of the brochure wave had occurred, and even Dr. Harrison gave me special treatment. I was given the assignment as lead writer for the company's oral contraceptive line. I had to learn a whole new therapeutic area. This wasn't as difficult as it sounds because the FDA requirements were the same no matter what the drug. I started my new assignment by doing a lot of background research. I'd sit in my office hours at a time reading through statistical reports, clinical study reports, protocols, and the Code of Federal Regulations. I knew I was a real science geek because I actually enjoyed this stuff. As I started focusing more and more on my work, I thought less and less of Jane. I realized that I didn't love her; she was only a diversion. I only got together with her once more in September. It was obvious to both of us that our initial chemistry was starting to fade.

It went on like this all through October, until things came to a head on Halloween. The day before Halloween, Jane informed me, "I'm going to a Halloween party with Joey."

Even though I knew it was coming, I was still upset. "You are going to a Halloween party with Joey the urban tracker? What am I supposed to do?"

"You know as well as I do that we're not right for each other," she said.

"Well, no couple is perfect together Jane," I retorted. "Joey and I have more in common than you and me," she said. I could tell from the first time they met that this was true.

I drove home and pouted the rest of the night. I had lost at serious relationship number two. All of my suspicions about Joey the urban tracker were true, or perhaps they were a self-fulfilling prophecy.

I had lost my second Philly girl and with her some of my luster at work. Bernie sensed that I had experienced some sort of emotional loss, but he really liked me and didn't want to pry. In addition, my new assignment at work was much more difficult than I originally anticipated. The intricacies of female hormones were amazing, and one could spend a lifetime trying to understand them. I just wanted to understand them enough to be able to do a good job at work. Dr. Harrison could tell that I was struggling a little bit, but he didn't say anything because even though I had lost some of my lusters, I was still too hot to touch.

During the next few weeks, I allowed myself a little time for retrospection. I had lost two good Philadelphia women, and perhaps it was time to look within to find the answers why. The first I had lost over educational issues; the second I had lost due to some callous remarks. I realized that I had the capacity to be a cad, something I intensely disliked about myself. Although I had the right job to obtain a wife, I saw that I really was not that mature and that I had a lot to learn about women. Understanding their hormones was one thing, understanding the flesh and bone human female human being was another.

I still had my nest high above Valley Forge Park, and I still had my job, but now I was without a woman in my life. At least I still had Max. I had told Max about me and Jane breaking up and about Jane and Joey. It seemed like Jane was making the rounds of all of Max's friends, and somehow he thought that was amusing. After thinking about it for a while, so did I.

Max himself had a new girlfriend named Sherrie. She was a waitress at the London Victory Club, and she was also going to school at night for her MBA. She was short, blond, and very pretty. Max was a very big man, but their size difference didn't seem to matter to either one of them. I was happy for Max and also optimistic that Sherrie may have some female friends to introduce me to.

Max, in addition to his smarts, was also a musician. He played the guitar quite well and he had a decent singing voice. He formed a trio with Dave and another friend of Dave's, and they called themselves Great Guise. Somehow, they got a gig at the London Victory Club, and on break, Max had met Sherrie. They had been going out for a couple of weeks when Max told me about it.

As it turned out, Sherrie was a rower for one of the university teams. She was on the water every morning by seven a.m. for practice. Max had never seen such discipline and dedication. He told me that this was one of the things that attracted her to him.

Great Guise had a standing gig at the London Victory Club every Friday, and while Max was singing Sherrie was waitressing. I usually hung around the back of the bar so that I could talk to Sherrie. One Friday, Sherrie told me about a friend she had, Lauren, who was getting her MBA from NYU. She described her as a short, blue-eyed brunette who was very serious about her career, and she was interested in meeting new men, as she had just broken up with her fiancée. She sounded like my type so I said I'd be interested in meeting her. Sherrie said she could probably arrange that.

With this news, I felt buoyant and wanted to get drunk. I continued to suck down beers and appreciate the vocal harmony of Great Guise until I had to stop if I wanted to get home. Lauren sounded perfect for me— ambitious, driven, pretty, and from a good family. Sherrie said she was going to try to arrange the meeting for next Friday. I had to wait a whole week just to meet her!

I was excited and curious at the same time. Who was this ambitious woman whose family was from the Main Line? I knew that I had to be on my best behavior to impress her, but further than that, I knew that I had to beef up my wardrobe. For this, I turned to Max. Max suggested going to The Men's Warehouse on Callow Hill Street.

I had about three hundred dollars to spend. With that, I was able to buy a gray Harris Tweed, a blue wool sports jacket, a pair of charcoal-colored wool pants, and five new silk ties. These were clothes that would help me fit right in on the Main Line. I could use these outfits for both works and play too. To meet Lauren, I thought I'd wear the Harris Tweed.

CHAPTER

The next week at work was particularly difficult. It was official: Bernie had been demoted to number two man under Dr. Harrison. We all knew it was coming; it was just a matter of when. At least Bernie didn't sulk. He knew he wasn't as well qualified as Dr. Harrison and he had to accept his fate.

I felt sorry for Bernie, but I also knew that I had to play the political game and start sucking up to Dr. Harrison more. I was loyal but not stupid.

Oral contraceptives are a complicated piece of work, what with the estrogens and progestins and other complicated hormones interacting with each other. I was still wading in this ocean of biochemistry trying to produce a decent clinical study report. It was coming together, but very slowly. Dr. Harrison knew that Bernie and me were friends, but so far he wasn't holding that against me.

While all this was going on, I was also full of anticipation to meet Lauren. From her description, it sounded like she was perfect for me. Still, one never knows until meeting the person whether there will be chemistry or not. Max built her up too, and Max wasn't easily impressed.

On Friday morning, I turned my assignment in and hoped for the best. I didn't know if I had done a good job or not, I just knew I had done the best job I could. If that wasn't good enough, so be it. I left work at five o'clock and drove home to put on my Harris Tweed outfit. Tonight is the night I was going to meet Lauren.

I arrived at the London Victory Club at seven, even though Lauren wouldn't be there and the band wouldn't start until nine. I did order a beer and made a note to myself that this would be my only drink before Lauren arrived. I didn't want to be drunk when she arrived.

The band arrived at eight to start setting up, and Sherrie came on duty. When they were done, they asked me how the sound system sounded and I said fine. Both Max and Sherrie were very excited for me. There was an impalpable trace of special energy in the air, and we were all somehow affected by it.

At quarter to nine, I started to get nervous and I ordered another beer. Great Guise was getting ready to play and Max took the microphone to introduce the band, and just at that moment Sherrie tapped my shoulder and she was standing there with her friend.

"This is Lauren," she said.

"So nice to meet you; please sit down," I said.

She was exactly as Sherrie had described her, and I could tell that the chemistry was mutual. After some small talk, we became quiet to listen to the band. I already had visions in my head of love and marriage, and I wondered if she was thinking the same thing.

She was interested in my career, and I told her I was a science writer for a pharmaceutical company. That really seemed to impress her. She was a systems analyst for an insurance company, but her real goal was to work for a big eight accounting firm. It was obvious that we were both ambitious, and that made us connect even more. She told me how exciting New York was, but I told her that I thought that Philadelphia was exciting enough.

It was clear that after a couple of hours that Sherrie had made a successful match. The chemistry was mutual and it was clear that we both wanted to see each other again. On this November night, love was in the air, and Great Guise amplified it. From the stage, Max could see that the introduction was successful, and Max smiled at me.

On break, Max and Sherrie came over and sat down next to us. They could tell that Lauren and me had "clicked," and they were talking about doing things as a foursome. By eleven o'clock, I knew that I was already in love with Lauren, and I held great expectations for things to come.

CHAPTER

With things improving on the personal front, things were also improving at work. Even though Bernie had lost all of his direct reports, he still had a lot of clout with the docs. Dr. Harrison was reveling in the fact that he was now the head of the department, but he still gave Bernie his due homage. Bernie had been responsible for setting up the computer system at work, a major accomplishment. He had also recruited half of the staff, including me, and so far all of us had been a success on the job. I was still plowing away at clinical study reports on oral contraceptives, and so far I had been doing a decent job. However, my assignments were becoming increasingly complex, and I didn't know how long I could keep up the good work.

Happiness on the personal front kept me bubbly at work, and that helped me tackle those difficult assignments. After a few days at work, I called Lauren and asked to see her next weekend. She was more than happy to hear from me, and she said yes.

Sometimes I wished I had a Ph.D. in science like Dr. Harrison, but I was successful enough with what I had. I didn't want to go back to school after all the education I already had. I had just spent seven years in college, and in my mind, that was enough. Not only was I tired of school, I was very happy with this accomplishment. I had already achieved more education than either of my parents, and I was proud of that. It was obvious that Lauren was success-driven too, and we had that in common.

I knew I had to be aggressive with Lauren or she would never be interested in me. How to be aggressive without chasing her away was a fine line. I decided that asking her on a trip with me might be the way to go. I was preoccupied with destinations at work for the next few days, and then it hit me on Thursday. I had a friend who I had grown up with who had moved to Paris, and he wasn't there right now he was in Germany on business. Perhaps I could borrow his apartment for a week. I decided to call him. He said no problem, he would send me the key in the mail and all I would have to pay for was airfare and food. If my second date with Lauren was a success, that's where I'd ask her to go with me.

For our second date, Lauren decided that we should go to a restaurant with Max and Sherrie. We decided on a place in Haverford called the Rusty Nail. It was a local hangout on the Main Line. On Friday night, we all met there and listened to a good rock and roll band. I gathered my courage and asked Lauren if she would come to Paris with me. Even though it was only our second date, she said yes. I was ecstatic. We had a wonderful time to plan. I told her about my friend and his apartment and that we could probably spend a week in Paris for under a thousand dollars, including air fare. Max and Sherrie were excited for us, and there was nothing that could interfere with our happiness.

When I got home, I called my friend in Paris and told him that the trip was a go. Half of the fun of a trip is the planning of it, and Lauren and I had a lot of planning to do. The first decision we had to make was which airline to book with. We found the cheapest airfare with Icelandic Air, only four hundred dollars apiece roundtrip. Icelandic Air actually flew to Luxembourg, but from there we could take the train to Paris. Direct flights to Charles De Gaulle airport were much more expensive. That was a no-brainer, and we called and made the reservation.

With another five hundred dollars, we could buy food and have enough money for miscellaneous expenses. We pooled our money and we had enough. The trip was a go!

The itinerary was set for April. What could be better than April in Paris? My friend sent me an excellent guide of what to see and do in Paris along with the key to his apartment.

At work, my star was back on the rise again. My enthusiasm was infectious, and people noticed a change in my demeanor at work. I was robust with enthusiasm. The word robust can be used to define a statistical equation, but it can also apply to human beings. It is a term that could be used to describe someone to whom no harm can come, where trouble bounces off him or her with ease. Such is the effect of love.

It is said that angels can walk on air, and people in love can walk on air too, at least in their imaginations. Such was the case for me. Female hormones were no longer a conundrum and everything I did meet with Dr. Harrison's approval.

I thanked my lucky stars that I had met someone like Lauren, and I was grateful to Max and Sherrie. Weeks went by in a hurry, and I was convinced that Lauren was the one for me. Somehow, I was going to climb the mountain and overcome the circumstances of my birth and create some magic.

At work, I kept my pencils sharp, my pens filled, and my hands clean. Bernie's star was fading so fast I had to keep a safe distance away. He had even lost his clout with the docs—I was on my own.

The key to my success in the next couple of months was to continually make Dr. Harrison happy and stay out of trouble. With a girl like Lauren in my life, it wasn't difficult to be the Teflon man. It was wonderful to feel things bounce off me with no energy expended. It is a phenomenon that should be scientifically analyzed someday, but this is neither the time nor the place for this discourse. Suffice it to say that love manifests itself in the world in strange ways, and one should approach it with wonder.

Love provides a benchmark below which no man or woman can descend. I was just starting to understand this wisdom just enough to know that I was not going to mess up my life between now and Paris. Perhaps the benchmark is confidence, I don't know, but I did know that I had enough confidence to make this current dream I was living a reality for at least the foreseeable future.

In order to stretch my budget in Paris, I picked up a copy of Down and Out in Paris and London by George Orwell. This little literary gem was a mainstay of how to survive in a big city on a small budget. Not only that, it also manages to be very funny even though the overall message is very sad.

After reading the book, I realized that it was no longer possible to survive on two or three francs a day or less like George Orwell did, but now I wondered if it was possible to live on twenty or thirty francs a day. Anyway, that became my goal.

I submitted my proposed budget to Lauren to see what she thought, and she thought it might be possible. After all, she should know more about budgets than me—she was the one studying for an MBA.

The currency exchange rate was three francs to the dollar, so we were looking at a budget of only ten dollars a day. Fortunately, this was just a goal, not an absolute. There would be additional expenses for trains and the metro, and we would have to stay away from fancy restaurants like Maxim's, for example. Souvenirs would have to be kept to a minimum, and I would have to go lightly on the cigarettes at five bucks a pack.

Lauren and I were now seeing each other two times a week, and all we did was plan our trip and our budget. There were numerous details to attend to, but as the week in April drew nearer, all of these sorted themselves out, and things seemed to go on autopilot. Without much time left, we were both getting pretty anxious and to put into practice what we had put on the drawing board.

CHAPTER

The thing that impresses one most about Luxembourg is the hills. If it weren't for the gothic cathedrals and the foreign language signs, one might think one was in Pittsburgh. We traipsed those hills and smelled the flowers, and both of these things were free.

After a few hours, we headed for the train station to catch our ride to Paris. Halfway through the journey, we stopped at Metz. There, they allowed passengers to get off the train for fifteen minutes. There was a patisserie at the train stop, and Lauren and I bought coffee and croissants for the equivalent of a few bucks. My croissant was chocolate, and hers was raspberry. We did not know the coffee brand, but it was strong.

Back on the train, we only had an hour left to Paris and we were both getting very excited. We finally arrived at the grand terminal, and we looked at our maps for the fourteenth arrondissement where our apartment was. We found the correct Metro stop and noted it on our map.

Once we got off our stop, we only had a block walk to the apartment. We arrived at the door and I got out the key. We opened the door. It was only a studio, but the bed looked comfortable and it was clean. Even Lauren wasn't disappointed. We threw our suitcases down and decided to go to the Eiffel Tower. Tulips were everywhere and we found a volunteer to take a picture of us with the Eiffel Tower in the background. This didn't cost a cent.

We walked through the Tuileries Gardens on our way to the Bois de Boulogne. Old French men were playing bocce in the park and we stopped for a few minutes to observe them. The Bois de Boulogne is a huge wilderness area on the west side of Paris, and it was a well-known trysting spot for lovers like us.

It was getting to be dusk, so we started walking east again towards our apartment. There was a brasserie, or café, on the corner of our street, and we were both pretty hungry so we decided to stop and hopefully have a cheap meal. We both ordered coffee and pizza, which we got away with for twenty francs each. This was the only meal we had all day, and we realized that we had come in under our thirty-franc a day budget and we were very happy.

We both awoke at dawn the next morning and we looked out through the window. The sun was coming up over Germany's horizon, and the red streaks of light were just reaching the streets. Today, we were traveling to Versailles, the home of the French kings. The train fare was only fifteen francs apiece. We reached the huge golden gates and took some pictures. Inside, we discovered the Hall of Mirrors and toured the bedroom of Louis XIV. Both were very impressive. But even more impressive than the mansion were the gardens and fountains behind the mansion. The main fountain is almost a mile long, and nestled in the woods at the end of it was Marie Antoinette's carriage house where she awaited execution after the French Revolution.

Since we were already halfway there, we decided to hop back on the train and go to the monastery on the coast known as Mont St. Michael. We got off the train and started walking the thousands of steps to the top. From there, we stared out over the English Channel and thought about all the centuries of history we were standing on. The air was so pure here that neither of us had ever smelled anything like it. We climbed back down and were headed for the train, but first, we stopped at a patisserie and bought some croissants and coffee. Heading back to Paris, the sun was sinking behind Mont St. Michael, which produced a rainbow of colors in the sky and on the surf. Neither one of us had ever seen such colors before.

Day number three was devoted to Notre Dame and the Louvre. We scampered up the steps of Notre Dame to the top. We looked at the gargoyles there and admired their combination of beauty and ugliness. From the roof, one could see Montmartre and the Seine below and it was one of the most beautiful sights I had ever seen. And best of all, it was free.

The Louvre was not free, but the entrance fee was nominal. One could spend weeks inside the Louvre and not see everything, but we gave it our best shot. We were in awe of the Venus de Milo, broken arms and all. The inscrutable smile on Mona Lisa perplexed us, but we could still appreciate her beauty.

After we had our fill of art, we strolled out onto the Place de la Concorde, sat on a bench, and just watched people. We could tell the other tourists from the natives because the tourists were always in a hurry and the natives weren't. Sitting there, we felt like we blended in with the natives, but in reality, the native ignored us. They instinctively knew we weren't one of them.

We just started walking and we came across a flea market somewhere near the George Pompidou Center. Everything from blankets to clothes was on sale. Even in fashionable Paris, there were those who were willing to bargain hunt. Some things are universal. I bought a bandana, and Lauren bought a blouse. We were close to Montmartre, so we started walking towards Sacre Coeur church at the summit of Montmartre. After circling through Place de Tertre where all the sidewalk artists worked, we saw an inviting restaurant on the way down the hill.

I ordered a coquelette, and Lauren ordered a steak. A strolling violinist played some Eastern European rhapsody and the setting couldn't have been more romantic. When our food arrived, my coquelette was the size of my fist, while Lauren had a delicious-looking steak covered in peppercorns. My coquelette was almost all bones and I could only find a bite of food, so Lauren shared her steak with me. That was the moment I knew I was going to ask her to marry me. The dinner cost almost fifty francs. So much for our budget.

There was only one way home, and that was through the Opera Quarter. We passed the big red windmill in front of the Moulin Rouge, where some transvestites were coming out onto the street. They really were quite a sight and Lauren and I said hello to them. We paused in front of Maxim's, where Lauren took a picture of me smoking my pipe. This was free while eating there would have blown our budget.

We stopped at the brasserie on our corner for a last snack before going to bed. By then, it was obvious that Lauren felt the same way about me as I felt about her. We went to sleep in each other's arms, knowing what was to come.

Somehow, we slept in late the next morning and didn't wake up until after ten o'clock. Perhaps we were feeling delayed jet lag. In any event, we went down to breakfast at our corner bistro and ordered croissants with coffee. Today, we wanted to explore the Left bank, where the Sorbonne was, and where a lot of university students and artists lived.

We took the Metro to Avenue de St. Germaine, got off, and started walking down the street. There were bookstores everywhere, and cheap restaurants priced for artists and students. We loved the bohemian feel of the place and wished we had brought a book along. We made comparisons between Paris' Left Bank and Philadelphia's Left Bank. Paris may have the Sorbonne but we have Penn, etc. It could not be argued that the Schuylkill was more beautiful than the Seine, but the argument could be made that West River Drive was more beautiful than the Avenue de St. Germaine.

This was our last day in Paris, and we soaked up all of the atmospheres we could to take home with us. The Paris that we had seen would always be a part of us, and none of these memories could ever be erased barring head injury. We were in love, and we both knew it, and we both felt so alive that the whole earth could fall away and we would still behold that love in each other's gaze.

The next morning we were on the train back to Luxembourg via Metz. The trains in Europe are so much more elegant than U.S. trains. We exchanged the rest of our currency in Metz back to U.S. dollars, and we bought coffee and croissants at our favorite spot in Metz.

Our flight wasn't until 5 p.m. local time, and we would be in Luxembourg by noon, so we had five hours to kill. We decided to kill them by strolling throughout the airport picking up souvenirs. We bought chocolate and postcards. Due to the six-hour time difference, we wouldn't land in Philadelphia until 11 a.m. Fortunately, neither one of us had to work that day, and we would have time to unpack and get settled before going back to work.

CHAPTER

Buoyant from my trip, I returned to work with renewed self-confidence. Co-workers liked my new persona, and there was an air of invincibility about me. Dr. Harrison welcomed me back, and Bernie was still subdued but happy to see me. All of the work on oral contraceptives that I had done had been approved by the docs, and Dr. Harrison was very happy with me. I would never ascend to the top of the corporate ladder with my qualifications, but I could become a valuable mid-level pharmaceutical employee. That was good enough for me. The thing rolling around in my mind was whether or not that would be good enough for Lauren.

Performance on the job was just as important as credentials, although only the best credentials could propel one to the very top. With my credentials, I could survive and perhaps attain middle management someday. This may not have been the most ambitious plan in the world, but there were worse.

I knew that given where I was, I was good enough to get Lauren to marry me. That was all that mattered right now. Focus on what I needed for the present—that was the road to success, or at least that's what my parents had always taught me. One thing at a time, one step at a time. For now, I was good enough; maybe tomorrow I wouldn't be, but right now I was good enough. Tomorrow will take care of itself.

Certain that I met all of Lauren's criteria for a suitable mate, the only thing that remained was the proposal. I started thinking about how and where to do it. I decided I didn't want to do it in public but in the privacy of my own apartment. After Paris, that was the only way to go.

I also wanted to do it while Paris was still fresh on our minds. I decided to do it after work on Wednesday when we usually got together. I would make it short, sweet, and simple. Of course, before I could do it I had to buy a ring.

I went down to Jeweler's Row and picked out what I thought was a beautiful ring. Lauren loved rubies, so why not get her a ruby engagement ring? I put it on credit and had it gift-wrapped. I knew what Lauren's answer would be—I knew she was in love with me.

All day Wednesday at work, I kept going over in my mind the exact words I would use. I finally decided on "Do you want to get married?" It used modern dialect and sounded much less formal than "Will you marry me?"

That evening, I let Lauren in and two minutes later I popped the question. She got flushed and said yes right away. Well, the course of my destiny was changed in that instant, but I knew it was changing in a wonderful direction.

The wedding was set for the heart of winter. We had plenty of time to plan everything because it was still spring. My status as fiancée gave me newfound confidence at work too. Bernie's star had fallen as far down as it could possibly go, and I felt sorry for him. He was already in his late forties with nowhere to go and all he could do was hang onto his job. I counted my blessings that I was only twenty-six and still had the potential to be a huge success. That's the thing about age—when you are young the sky is the limit, but when you are middle-aged gravity has been working on you for so long that even your dreams are tainted. I would sit in Bernie's office for hours at a time trying to cheer him up. I would always be loyal to him because he had given me my first job in the industry and the golden brochure assignment. I would never forget that, and because of this, I would commiserate with him for as long as we both stayed at the same company.

I invited both Dr. Harrison and Bernie to my wedding—I was covering all by bases. In the meantime, I was given a new therapeutic area to work in—psychotropics. I had a lot to learn about the human brain.

The next few months raced by and details of the wedding consumed Lauren. Fortunately for me, she was doing most of the work and I was able to focus on my job. Before we knew it, it was the day of the rehearsal. Afterward, Lauren was sick and was late to the rehearsal dinner. I wondered if she was getting cold feet, but she was her usual bubbly self when she finally did arrive at the restaurant.

I had to ask for help from my parents to cover the cost of the rehearsal dinner. Dinner for thirty people cost over a thousand dollars, and I just didn't have the money. This was also the night of my bachelor's party, and after the rehearsal dinner was over, my friends took me to the only strip club on the Main Line in Haverford. I proceeded to get quite drunk, but I wasn't worried because the wedding wasn't until two days later.

The next morning Lauren called me at 11:00 a.m. and I was still in bed with a hangover. She was a little perturbed, but after apologizing she forgave me. I asked her if she was over her pre-marriage jitters, and she said yes.

The actual wedding was beautiful but short. Lauren looked beautiful in her mother's white wedding dress, and I looked like Cary Grant in my black tux. During the whole wedding and the reception I was in a daze and both events were somehow surreal to me. Suddenly, we were at the Dupont Hotel to spend our first honeymoon night, and although we made love it was pretty lackluster because we were both so exhausted.

We didn't begin to really have fun on our honeymoon until the next day when we drove south to Williamsburg, Virginia. Colonial Williamsburg in the snow was beautiful, and since we were both history majors, we both felt the history of the place.

Besides the wonderful food and accommodations, what made Williamsburg special were the colonial artisans.

They all made products the way they were made more than two hundred years ago, and it was fascinating to watch. During our five days there, we got to see most of them at their craft and we really did feel like we were catapulted back in time. Although our love was just starting out, we knew what we appreciated in each other, and that alone was a solid foundation.

CHAPTER

ack at work in the real world, we had thank you
letters to write to all of our wedding guests. Some
of the presents we had received were very
beautiful and expensive. I was given half the list. I put their
addresses on my word processor at work to make the job
easier. This took several hours, but nobody at work
noticed.

Lauren wondered how I had finished my list so soon,
and when I told her she was a little upset with me. "Don't
you go jeopardizing your job over personal chores," she
said. I didn't realize how much she cared about my job
until then.

At work, I was still plowing through the world of brain
chemistry, learning everything there was to know about
serotonin, dopamine, and the other neurotransmitters. My
assignment was to work on clinical study reports for a new
anti-depressant, Zosoft. It was one of a new class of drugs
known as selective serotonin reuptake inhibitors or SSRIs.

Bernie had been demoted to the third circle of work Hell writing standard operating procedure manuals. I felt so sorry for him, but I couldn't let it show because it might affect my performance. I still went out to lunch with him, but as soon as we got back in the office I kept my distance.

I was put on the "A" team to work on Zosoft. We all had the right advanced degrees and the best reputations in the department. There wasn't a slacker in the group. We were the golden boys and girls of clinical writing.

Everyone in the group was aware of my fiancée's status, and they were all warm and friendly to me. I began to realize that the company valued men who had women in their lives a little bit more than the loner bachelors. Perhaps it was because it gave them a little more stability, I don't know, but my status was definitely higher than the unattached guys.

I told Lauren about my new therapeutic area and she was very happy for me because she knew how difficult the oral contraceptive work had been for me. She was even more happy when I told her I was working with the "A" team. Lauren had high aspirations for my career and this made her very happy indeed.

For her part, the engagement had to be good for Lauren too because she had been promoted from systems analyst one to systems analyst two at her insurance company. She was struggling with a few of her MBA classes, but she told me it was nothing she couldn't handle. Working all day and then going to business school at night was difficult enough, but when you add in that it was NYU in New York, it becomes more than difficult. I was glad that my life was being lived in the more subdued town of Philadelphia.

Of course, Lauren had put her studies on hold to come live with me in Philadelphia. We found an apartment in an apartment building in Bryn Mawr, the heart of the Main Line. It was small, but we furnished it nicely and it was convenient to everything. In fact, the only negative thing about our apartment was that we had an alcoholic maintenance man. Every time we saw him he would he fixing something, and his breath would reek of alcohol. He was nice enough, and maybe he thought we wouldn't notice, but he was certainly drunk almost every day. He was in his mid-forties and very thin, and it was obvious that his station in life didn't allow him to have a woman. Lauren would constantly cut him down and make fun of him, but I felt sorry for him.

One day while he was out mowing the apartment complex lawn, he pushed his lawnmower straight into a tree and broke the motor. He started cursing and broke into a sweat. He pulled out his flask and started emptying it just as Lauren looked out our window to what had caused the noise. She called me over to observe the scene and I just chuckled. Lauren took it seriously, however, and said she was going to do everything in her power to get him fired. That was the first moment that I realized that Lauren had the potential to be a real bitch.

CHAPTER

We all aspire to something, and my aspiration was to be a top-notch medical writer. Some people never accomplish their aspirations, but I had accomplished mine by the age of twenty-seven. I was proud of what I had accomplished, and even though I had a secret artistic streak, I was able to overcome it and not live like an artist.

Certain things that I did and said made Lauren suspicious about me possibly having an artistic streak, but I never did anything overtly to confirm her suspicions. Now that I had witnessed her bitch potential, I knew that I had to do everything I could to keep my artistic streak in check. The Main Line and artistry do not go hand in hand.

I was cruising along with the "A" team at work and keeping my nose clean. I got an occasional perk through my job such as a training session off campus, and when these occurred I usually partied it up.

Lauren didn't seem to enjoy the details of my work, only my status within the department. I told her I didn't think I would be getting another promotion for quite some time as I had just received one, but that didn't stop her from pushing. I started to resent her for that.

For her part, her promotion boosted her self-confidence to the point where she started dreaming really big. She started having visions of making partners of a big eight accounting firm. She pooh-poohed those of her colleagues with lesser ambition and considered herself a class above them. Her hautie-tautie attitude was beginning to grate on my nerves. I began to wonder how long she would be content to be married to a lowly medical writer and not a corporate mogul. These were my incipient fears, and I started hoping that things would start to go in a different direction.

Although Lauren was having these lofty visions, she was still a woman with maternal instincts. We decided to get a puppy. We drove to the King of Prussia pet shop and started looking around. After looking at beagles and Jack Russell terriers we were still undecided. Then a pet shop worker brought us to a pen at the front of the store that we had missed. Inside were fluffy little balls of white and tan. They were newborn peek-a-poo's, a cross between a Pekinese and a poodle. At that moment, one little fluffball looked right at us and started walking toward us inside the pen.

"We'll take him," Lauren said with delight. He was two hundred and fifty dollars but Lauren was in heaven. We also bought door fences, a bed, food and water bowls, a leash, and food. Altogether, we spent well over three hundred dollars. When we got home, we decided to name him Mochi, because his fur was the color of mocha.

Since we both worked, we left Mochi in the kitchen with newspapers on the floor. We were hoping that it would only take a few months to train him. In addition, Mochi was teething, and when we let him run loose he would go straight for the shoelaces on my shoes. There must be something about leather that dogs can pick up on dog radar.

One weekend, we took Mochi to Reservoir Park. We walked on a long wharf that stretched out over the water. When we reached the end, for some reason Mochi jumped off the wharf into the water. Being a puppy, he didn't know how to swim and started sinking immediately. There was no time to think—I jumped into the water fully clothed. I found him about two feet below the surface and I grabbed him and pulled him to the surface. I could see the look of relief on Lauren's face as I started swimming with one arm towards the end of the wharf. I reached up and put Mochi on the wharf and then I hoisted myself up.

For a few moments, I was Lauren's superhero. Then she realized how stupid it was to let Mochi anywhere near the end of the wharf. I pulled out my wallet and all my money was soaking wet, but I was consoled by the fact that once it dried it was still legal tender. Lauren wanted to get back home so that we could dry Mochi off with a hairdryer.

CHAPTER

Now that there was a certain amount of domesticity in my life at home, my work life seemed to be rolling along more smoothly. Those on the "A" team were recognized as the aces in the department, and kudos followed us around as though we all had halos. Dr. Harrison was still the high science priest, but as his special acolytes, we were treated with reverence as well. In fact, the only member of the department who wasn't treated with reverence was Bernie. His fall from grace was now complete. It was Bernie's education that did him in. All he had was a two-year LPN degree from a local college, and he got that through the GI bill. Mater's and Ph.D. scientists were just too far better educated than he was for him to be their boss. The law of business natural selection had manifested itself in his fall from number one to number two to the bottom. What I couldn't stand was the abuse that went with his new position in life. He now was working on quality assurance guidelines, the netherworld of the corporate kingdom. Not only was the work boring, but there was no escaping it except by divine edict. Bernie was now in chains in the bottom hold of the ship. All I could do to cheer him up was visit him and tell a few jokes. I could tell how much he appreciated that feeble gesture.

Things went on like this for several months, and then by some miracle things took a different turn. Dr. Harrison hired another Ph.D. scientist by the name of Dylan Scott. After a few weeks, it became apparent that Dr. Scott and Bernie had bonded and become fast friends. In an amazing coincidence, Dr. Scott had moved into the apartment next to Lauren and me. I was becoming friends with Dylan Scott too.

Becoming friends with Dr. Scott lifted Bernie's spirits tremendously. Dr. Scott's credentials were so unassailable that he knew that as long as he did his job he could hang out with anybody he chose to—even Bernie. The three of us formed a sort of renegade trinity. We were the oddballs of the department. Dylan was ten years younger than Bernie and I was ten years younger than Dylan. A decade for medical writers may as well be a generation, so we were a three-generation partnership.

Dylan's wife worked for a marine insurance company. Her name was Surran and she was of Lebanese descent. She was very pretty with brown eyes and long black hair.

One day, Bernie, Dylan, and I were sitting in Dylan's apartment, and Dylan pulled out some pot and we all got stoned. On his kitchen counter were some pictures of a Caribbean vacation Dylan had taken—with another woman. Dylan told Bernie he had gone there with his lab assistant—Puffy Mew—daughter of one of the wealthiest families in Philadelphia. Bernie couldn't believe Dylan's carelessness in leaving the pictures on the kitchen counter. What if Surran saw them? Dylan said he didn't care, that he was already planning on leaving Surran for Puffy. Bernie convinced Dylan to hide the pictures in a cookie jar, that it wasn't fair of Dylan to leave them out in the open. Dylan finally conceded and put the pictures away.

A few days later, I told Lauren the story and she said she wasn't sure if we should be friends with Dylan anymore. I told her that no matter what happened I would always be loyal to Dylan because I valued his friendship at work. Besides that, he was irresistibly funny.

About a week later, the shit hit the fan. One night, Surran discovered the pictures in the cookie jar. We could hear the screaming from our apartment. We could hear Surran crying and screaming at the same time, and finally, the door slamming and loud footsteps down the hall. We assumed it was Surran that left.

It was a few weeks before Christmas, and the Wyatt Christmas party was coming up. Dylan was very subdued at work and barley opened his mouth. Even though he was the one leaving his marriage, he was still in deep pain. Bernie and I took Dylan out to lunch every day just to be there for him, and we could tell that he was very appreciative. Even though Bernie was at the bottom of the corporate ladder, he was no longer at the top of the emotional pain scale—Dylan was.

Bernie, Dylan, and I made plans to go to the Christmas party together. It was being held at a swank hotel on the Main Line. There was a free open bar, and Bernie and Dylan were throwing drinks down like there was no tomorrow. After an hour of free drinks and free hors d'oeuvres, Dylan and Bernie were quite drunk. The three of us stepped outside for a smoke. An ice storm the previous night had left a sheet of ice on the ground and it was very slippery.

Halfway through our cigarette break, Dylan saw Dr. Harrison walking towards us. All of a sudden, Dylan started swearing at Dr. Harrison. His face was completely red and he was obviously out of control. Dylan took a swing at Dr. Harrison, which he easily evaded by leaning backward. Dylan's inertia caused him to do a three-sixty on the ice during which he lost his balance and smashed his head on the ice. Blood started spurting out of the wound, and Bernie and I had to take him to the hospital for stitches. Such was the Christmas party of 1983.

The next week, Dylan showed up to work with a big white bandage on his head. But the absolutely amazing thing was that Dr. Harrison didn't fire him. Unbelievably, it was business as usual and Dylan didn't say a word about it and neither did Dr. Harrison. Bernie and I concluded that there must be some sort of mysterious mutual respect that we didn't understand.

When I told Lauren that Dylan had evidently been forgiven she couldn't believe it. She had lost all respect for Dylan after what he had done to his wife, and now she felt uncomfortable just living next to him. She started looking in the real estate section of the paper at townhouses.

Real estate agents on the Main Line can be very accommodating when there is money to be made. Being young nesters, we didn't have a lot of money, so we had to look at lowto middle-priced townhouses. We saw one that we liked in Wayne—a three-story townhouse right behind Minerva's diner. We put a bid on it and surprisingly the owner accepted it. We were now almost homeowners! It was fairly large, and we would have to buy additional furniture to furnish it properly. This was clearly Lauren's department, and I gave her free reign. She not only had better taste than me, but she also knew where to shop. Everything she bought was expensive, of course, but we both had good incomes and liked quality merchandise.

After settlement, Lauren marked off each day on the calendar closer to move day. She couldn't wait to get away from both our alcoholic caretaker and Dylan. When move day finally arrived, she was beaming with excitement and pride. I liked her best when she was in this mood.

I particularly liked being within close proximity of Minerva's diner. The food was good and cheap and a relief from the usual Main Line prices. Mochi seemed to like his new habitat, and it gave him a good workout too with the two flights of stairs. There were only eight units in our complex, which gave it a sense of intimacy. All of our neighbors were very friendly, and they all welcomed us to the neighborhood.

Lauren was glad to be away from Dr. Scott, and quite frankly, so was I. Dr. Scott was getting bored with his job and his tenure at Wyatt Laboratories was in jeopardy. There was no sense in buddying up to him at work anymore. He made it clear that he had put his resume on the market and that he would probably be leaving as soon as the first good offer came around.

Dr. Scott was from Maine, and before leaving there he had bought an oyster farm. He left a manager in charge of it when he left, but his dream was to grow rich through this oyster farm. Dylan called Maine several times a week on company time, and finally, Dr. Harrison noticed the long-distance telephone bills. Finally, there was something tangible for Dr. Harrison to use against Dylan. He called Dylan into his office and chewed him out. Dylan left the office in a huff.

The next day, Dylan showed up at work with a gun and holster and he hung it on his coat rack in plain sight.

In a quiet voice, he told me it was only a bee bee pistol, but he hoped it would scare Dr. Harrison.

If he saw it, Dr. Harrison didn't say anything. The gun and holster just sat there on the coat rack for several days—and nothing happened. Only Bernie, Dylan, and I seemed to be aware of its existence.

Towards spring, Dylan decided that he needed to visit his oyster farm for some reason. Bernie and he were planning to go together and make it a real road trip. Bernie was so excited he could hardly contain himself.

When that week arrived, I had never felt so alone at work. Bernie and Dylan provided all of my social life at work, and without them, work was dull. My other colleagues noticed how somber I was, and they all knew why. I was pretty disappointed that Bernie and Dylan didn't ask me to go with them, but the truth of the matter is that I didn't have the vacation time to spare anyway. All I knew was that if Dylan left the company, Bernie would probably retire and I would be left alone to fend for myself.

I told all this to Lauren and she suggested that I should start polishing my resume too. Deep in my heart, I knew that she was right.

CHAPTER

Sure enough, Dylan gave his resignation to Dr. Harrison the next week. He had been offered a job at Dupont Pharmaceuticals. Bernie was devastated when Dylan told him the news. His salvation from being demoted was soon to be over. I knew that once our triumvirate was over, things would never be the same. I had a few nibbles on my resume already.

On Dylan's last day, Bernie and I took him out to lunch. Dylan told us that he had asked Puffy to marry him and she had said yes. He invited us to his wedding. It was apparent that Bernie's and Dylan's friendship would survive Dylan's departure from Wyatt Laboratories. This invitation to Dylan's wedding cheered Bernie up to no end.

The next week, with Dylan gone, Bernie was back in Hell. It was obvious after a few days that Dr. Harrison was going to torture Bernie for befriending a traitor. For some reason, possibly because of my youth, I was forgiven.

Lauren thought that I should keep my distance from Bernie. I just couldn't do it though because I liked him so much.

Patiently I waited to hear something from the recruiter who I had sent my resume to. Finally, by the end of the week, I had heard something—Phitzer Laboratories in New York City was interested in me. They needed an in-house clinical research associate and they thought I fit the bill. The interview was set for Friday of the next week.

When I told Lauren the news, she was ecstatic because she always wanted to go to New York. I knew she would be happy, but I didn't expect the effusion of emotion that I received. She prepped me for the interview by buying me a new watch and a new suit. I knew then that she really wanted me to get this job.

I confided in Bernie about my interview and he wished me luck. He thought that moving on was probably a good idea. I thanked him for giving me my start in the industry and asked him if I could treat him to lunch. I took him to the bar/restaurant that we always went to and we ordered a couple of beers. I realized that Bernie's star had already fallen and mine was just beginning to rise. I thought to myself God bless youth.

I took the train to New York and arrived at Penn Station by ten a.m. I hailed a cab and told the driver that I needed to go to forty-second and third. Weaving in and out traffic, I arrived there by ten thirty. My interview wasn't until eleven o'clock. I waited in the reception area for Dr. Margolis. Precisely at eleven, he came walking out and shook my hand.

I showed him my portfolio and I could tell that he was impressed. He liked my personality and I told him both my wife and myself wanted to go to New York. He asked me the routine questions which I answered satisfactorily, and I knew the job was in the bag—it was mine if I wanted it. On the train back to Philadelphia, I was already thinking about where in New York I wanted to live. Perhaps Lauren had some idea about that.

The only problem was money. It took a lot more money to live in New York than it did to live in Philadelphia. I would have to ask for at least a twenty percent increase in salary or it wouldn't be worth the move. That would only be the minimum, of course. I would now be in competition with Wall Street investment bankers and corporate moguls. Lauren and I were both young urban professionals, and we should be able to make enough money to live well. Secretly, however, I thought I would fit in better with the bohemians of Greenwich Village than the super sharks on Wall Street. Of course, I could never let Lauren know this.

Over the next few weeks, Lauren and I planned two trips to New York to look at real estate. For the first visit, we decided to look at houses in Westchester County. For the second visit, we would look in north Jersey.

On the very first day of our trip to Westchester, our real estate agent found us a little Cape Cod that we both fell in love with. We knew we didn't need to look any further. It was exactly what we needed and were looking for. We figured we should make a twenty thousand dollar profit on our townhouse, and that should cover our deposit.

The next week we heard the word—I had gotten the job at Phitzer. Everything was a go. We put our townhouse up for sale and we told our agent in New York to put a bid on the Cape Cod.

Lauren was so excited she could barely contain herself. New York had always been her final destination and now things were finally falling into place for her. Things were falling into place for me too because I loved it when Lauren was excited. We started planning the move and with it a new life in New York.

CHAPTER

26

Central Park is a joke compared to Fairmount Park, Washington Park is a joke compared to Washington Square, and Herald Square is a joke compared to Rittenhouse Square. In my estimation, the Free Library of New York is a joke compared to the Free Library of Philadelphia. The only thing that isn't a joke is the Metropolitan Museum of Art, but even that isn't as nice as the Philadelphia Art Museum.

There are approximately eight million people living in the New York metropolitan area, compared to only four million in the metropolitan Philadelphia area, but in my opinion, Philadelphia is much nicer and much cheaper. Of course, New York is the corporate capital of the world, the Big Apple, the city that never sleeps. My idea was to stay in New York for a few years, making the big bucks, and then head back to Philadelphia. I wasn't sure if that was Lauren's plan or not. For my taste, there were too many foreigners in New York. I was just getting used to the ethnic diversity of Philadelphia, and now I had to deal with New York. We would be somewhat isolated from the poverty of the majority living in Westchester County, but there were more homeless in New York than in Philly and more beggars hanging out on the streets.

There was also much more attitude in New York than in Philly. The streets were meaner and the people were tougher. The accents were also much more acute than in Philadelphia, especially the Brooklyners. Besides that, just about every language in the world was spoken in New York.

What really put New York on a different scale than Philadelphia though was the competition—eight million people scrambling over each other to get ahead. I knew I could only take it for a few years while I was young, and then I would have to get out because I wasn't raised to it. I wasn't sure if Lauren felt that way or not. New York was a sea of skyscrapers in which people served capitalism. And some people served it better than others. I realized that in the great scheme of things, I was average at it.

We moved into our Cape Cod in the middle of the summer. In our back yard were tall maple trees and on the fence that surrounded the pool huge clematis flowers dangled at every angle. The pool was kidney-shaped and not very big, but from our sunroom, it looked quite pretty. We had a little slice of nature's paradise right in our own backyard. It was a necessary retreat from the harshness of our days.

At Pfitzer, it was like there were a thousand mad scientists running around. Superegos were everywhere; fortunately for me, Dr. Margolis was not one of them. He was practical and down-to-earth and very nice. He praised me whenever I did a good job on something, and he was kind when I made a mistake. In return, I kept my artistic streak on a short leash and never questioned his judgment.

Because of its scale, even though public transportation was easy, it took longer because New York was bigger. It took me exactly one hour to get to work from door to door. It took Lauren slightly longer.

When it came to food, New York may have a slight edge on Philadelphia, the main reason being the delis. New York delis have more food than I had ever seen and it was relatively cheap. New York restaurants were famous, but you had to pay through the nose. Even the street food in New York was better than in Philadelphia. The street hot dog vendors sold not only franks but Italian sausage and Polish sausage as well. All in all, however, I liked the geography of Philadelphia much better than New York. I missed the winding curves of Philadelphia as opposed to the squareness of everything in New York. As we settled into our new routines, we realized that we had to spend more hours at work and less time having fun, and I wasn't happy with this new direction we were heading in.

We decided to strive to have more fun. Thursday nights we declared to be city night. We chose a different restaurant every week until we had covered the whole city. One week it was Chinatown, the next week it was Little Italy, and so on until we had eaten all over the city.

Our favorite Chinese restaurant was Wo Hops. From the outside, it was a hole in the wall, but inside were endless subterranean caverns where food was served. My favorite dish was crab in black bean sauce. It was so delicious it was indescribable. Everything was good there, but this dish truly was something special. Lauren wasn't crazy about shellfish; otherwise, she would have loved it too. We tried to go there at least once a month.

In addition, we tried Thai restaurants, Korean restaurants, Indian restaurants, Hungarian restaurants, Moroccan restaurants, French restaurants, Greek restaurants, English restaurants, and Spanish and Portuguese restaurants. The miracle of all this is that we didn't gain any weight. If we had been in our late thirties instead of our late twenties we probably would have.

Besides the restaurants, there was always wonderful music. We never saw a bad band in the Village, and if we wanted classical there was always the Metropolitan Opera and the New York Philharmonic. There was also Carnegie Hall. Somebody famous was always there every week.

New York was also home to many celebrities. In our first few months there, we saw Woody Allen, Robert De Niro, Matthew Modine, and Leslie Nielson. Of course, if the good life could be had on a grander scale in New York than in Philadelphia so could the downside. The New York Mob was much more ruthless than the Philly Mob, and only New York could create a Michael Milken, the junk bond king. Here, white-collar crime was considered much more than petty theft, and the ultimate white-collar crime was insider trading. People with big money made big money by listening to insiders' tips, and if you were caught you could go to prison. Isn't America great?

In my own immediate world, what concerned me most was how I was going to compete with the superbrains at Phitzer Laboratories. They weren't just extremely well educated; many of them were truly brilliant. My brain cells felt like they notched themselves up a notch just being around them, but I was worried about the long-term consequences of trying to keep up with them.

For her part, Lauren was up against some big guns too. It seemed like everybody in New York had advanced degrees up the wazoo, and only the people with the right pedigree made it to the very top. The right pedigree included an Ivy League degree, of course. In essence, New York was filled with thousands of bums and thousands of superachievers. By virtue of my job, I was living in the world of the superachievers, and so was Lauren. But just beneath the surface lay the underbelly of New York—the pimps and prostitutes, the Mob, the poor immigrants who couldn't speak a word of English, and the street criminals. New York had a lot of everything—a disproportionate amount of rich, a lot of poor, and millions in between.

CHAPTER

After a few months of getting acclimatized to New York, Dr. Margolis said he wanted to send me to a medical information meeting in London. When I got home and told Lauren the news, she was very excited and started planning a vacation around the trip. She wanted to spend a week seeing London and another week seeing the rest of the country. The trip would take up most of September, which we thought would be a fine time to see England. Of course, I would be there a week earlier to attend the conference.

I got my airline tickets a week before the trip—I was flying British Airlines since the company was paying for the trip. I got Lauren British Airlines tickets too. We got a deal on them because we were staying more than two weeks. By this time, Lauren had the whole trip planned. She would meet me in my hotel in London the day after the conference.

I arrived at Heathrow and took a cab to the White House Hotel just off Hyde Park. I checked into my room and put my luggage away. The conference didn't start until the next day so I decided to take an impromptu walking tour. Since Hyde Park was just across the street, I decided to start there.

After starting my walk, my first observation was that Hyde Park was huge. I had been walking for more than ten minutes, and I still couldn't see the end of the park. The other thing I observed is that the English know how to maintain a park. There wasn't one piece of litter on the ground, and the flowers were beautiful. After walking in the same direction for another ten minutes on the foot trail, I realized I'd have to cut back straight through the park to get back to my hotel or I would be out here forever. I did this and arrived at the White House in twenty minutes.

One other person from my department—Mary—had also been sent by the company to the conference. I called her from my room to see if she wanted to have dinner with me. She said O.K.

We met at seven at the hotel restaurant. I had put on a sports jacket to look more "professional." Mary was excited about the conference that started tomorrow too. After we ordered steaks, she kicked off one of her shoes and started rubbing her foot against my calf. She knew I was married, but it didn't deter her. I finished eating in a hurry, threw down a ten-pound note, and excused myself. This was the first time I had been propositioned since I had gotten married. I decided that I would avoid her the week of the conference.

During the conference, I learned one thing. English scientists are the best scientists in the world. English scientists had developed the first beta-blocker, the first antibiotic, the first proton pump inhibitor, and the first ace inhibitor. And the best thing about them was that they're all nice as hell.

After each day's sessions, they took me out drinking every evening. We tried a different pub every night, and by the last day, I could understand even the thickest English accent. I only ran into Mary twice the whole week, and I made it clear she had committed a faux pas.

The last day of the conference, with my head filled with scientific factoids, I was finally beginning to look forward to having Lauren join me in London. I figured she was probably getting ready to head to the airport just about now, and I couldn't wait to see her.

I slept in the morning of Lauren's arrival, and I awoke to the sound of the phone. Lauren was already at Heathrow and was on her way here. I jumped in the shower and got ready, heading down to the lobby around eleven a.m. local times.

I saw Lauren's cab pull up to the front doors of the hotel, and I got up to kiss her and help with her luggage. She was so happy to see me, and she looked great in a blue skirt and white blouse. We carried her luggage up to the room, and even though she wasn't crazy about the room she did like the hotel. She wanted to get going sightseeing right away, so she went to the bathroom and then we headed out to see London.

We walked to the Highchapel "tube" stop and headed south. We got off at Westminster Bridge. For London, it was a spectacularly sunny day. We walked to the south side of the bridge and looked back at Big Ben. Then we walked back across the bridge and toured Westminster Abbey. We were both fascinated by all the tombs of kings and queens and poets buried there.

From there, we walked over to The Tower of London. Inside were the Crown Jewels of England. We had never seen so many jewels in our life. After that, we went to St. Paul's Cathedral. By then, it was already dark and we got to see St. Paul's at night. The lights cast a greenish glow over the promontory it sat on and on the water of the Thames. We decided to call it a day and headed back north to our hotel. We had dinner in a small Indian restaurant down the street and decided to go to Buckingham Palace the next day.

Fortunately for us, the sun was shining the next day and we looked forward to another day in the sun. We were impressed with the redness of the uniforms of the guards. The horses of the mounted guards were also exquisite. The mounted guards wore long red frocks that flowed over the horses' backs. From there, we walked east to Trafalgar Square. We weren't that impressed with it, so we hopped a double-decker bus to take a motorized tour of the city.

The bus drove over Westminster Bridge and headed west along the Thames, and we got a beautiful view of the

House of Commons and Parliament. The bus drove right past Madam Toussaud's Wax Museum and we wanted to see it so we got off the bus and went inside. Lauren took a picture of me standing next to Alfred Hitchcock, and I took a picture of Lauren standing behind Joan Collins. Then I took another picture of Lauren standing amidst the royal family, and Lauren took a picture of me standing next to Humphrey Bogart in a white tux. Here's looking at you kid.

For the afternoon, we decided to spend our time in the gardens, first in Kensington Gardens and then in Hyde Park. The Kensington Gardens surrounded Buckingham Palace and they were beautiful, but I preferred Hyde Park. The banks of flowers in Hyde Park were so spectacular that we lingered every few moments to appreciate them. We determined that we had enough for one day and headed back to the hotel to have dinner. I told Lauren about the conference.

We started the next day by going to the British Museum. We were fascinated by the Egyptian and Greek and Roman relics. History came alive as we toured the galleries. After we were done with the British Museum, we walked south to Piccadilly Circus and the statue of Eros, and finally, we found our way to Harrod's department store. It was interesting to see the English taste in elegance, and we certainly found it here. It was starting to get dark and we were getting hungry so we decided to eat at a restaurant called the English House. The food was very English, but it wasn't too bad.

We bought tickets to see Starlight Express—the play that took place on roller skates—at the Apollo Victoria Theater in the West End, so we jumped into a cab. The play was fabulous and was different from anything we had ever seen.

The music, by Andrew Lloyd Webber, is what made the production so wonderful. Exuberant from the experience, we walked out onto the street and decided to see if we could walk all the way home. We actually got about halfway and were too tired to go on. We hailed a cab back to our hotel, and we fell asleep as soon as our heads hit the pillows.

Day 4 we devoted to Windsor Castle. We got on the train by nine a.m. and headed the twenty miles west. I had on my favorite blue sweater and Lauren had on a red blouse. There was so much history here we didn't know where to start. Stupidly, I didn't put on an overcoat and after several hours it looked like rain. Lauren, always prepared, wore her tan trench coat.

We knew it would take all day to see everything inside the castle and all the grounds. The statues were awe-inspiring and the grounds were so impressive we couldn't stop gawking.

Just outside the grounds of Windsor Palace was Eton, where schoolboys had been prepped for an elite life for centuries. It was really a quaint little village, with beautiful views of the Thames. We walked into a restaurant, and for some reason, I was in a very pensive mood. I ordered a beer and then assumed the pose of The Thinker by Paul

Rodin. Lauren took a picture of me in this pose, and she probably wondered what was going on in my head. I also had my glasses on, which amplified the effect I was trying to achieve. Between my glasses and my mustache and my fist covering my mouth, if she didn't know I was an intellectual by now, she never would. It was getting dark, so after eating we headed back to the train. We had taken two rolls of pictures just of Windsor Palace and Eton.

The next day, we decided we wanted to see the North Country. We boarded a train to Edinburgh early in the morning. Amazingly, the route northward followed the eastern coast of Britain, and we got to see some beautiful vistas of the English coastline. First, we went through Stratford-upon-Avon, then York, then Newcastle, and finally Edinburgh. Along the way, we saw Durham Cathedral and Hampton Court. We took pictures of these through our window, and they actually turned out pretty good.

After checking into the Royal Scots Hotel in Edinburgh and putting our luggage away, we wanted to see Holyrood Palace up close. This was the palace where the royal family always stayed when they were in Scotland. What struck me as most odd was the color of the bricks. They were a color of beige and tan that I had never seen before. After that, we returned to town and did High Street's historic mile. Finally getting hungry, we headed back to our hotel. We ordered the traditional Scottish meal—haggis—and washed it down with some Scotch. It was getting late and we decided to get to bed because there was so much more we wanted to see the next day.

We spent the next day looking out over the vistas of Edinburgh Castle. We couldn't believe how high some of the ramparts were, and we wondered how they ever built the place. Coming down from the castle, we ventured onto some side streets and found that there were bars everywhere. Evidently, the Scottish like to drink! Who'd of thunk it?

We stopped in one of them and ordered beer. It was a good stopping point and we enjoyed the rest. Lauren was counting the money we had left and she told me we had to stop at a bank. We were down to our last few notes and we hadn't eaten dinner yet. We found an exchange bank and converted some currency. We stopped in a little restaurant close to our hotel and had our last dinner in Edinburgh. Once again, we ordered haggis because we had enjoyed it so much the previous night. We went to bed that night full of gratefulness for Phitzer giving us the time of our lives.

The next day it was time to head back down south, but we decided to spend a day in York. The original wall that fortified the city was still there, and tourists were able to walk on it. We got a passerby to take a photograph of us on top of the wall, and we both looked pretty good in it. After that, we walked along the Ouse River, and then toured the ruins of St. Mary's Abbey. We also toured the ruins of York Castle. The most famous restaurant in York was the Shambles, and we went there for dinner. After dinner, we decided we wanted to see more of Scotland, so we took a train back north the next day.

Bright and early, we headed for the train. We took the train past Edinburgh to Callandar and got off. We decided to spend the day climbing the crags of Scotland. Everywhere we looked was a beautiful vista. The geography of Scotland is unique, and we loved every new vista we came to.

After hiking all morning, we finally made it back to the train station by lunchtime and headed back to Edinburgh. We spent the rest of the day touring Holyrood Palace and St. Margaret's Abbey. We visited all over the grounds, which we thought was even more beautiful than Windsor palace because of the gorgeous mountains in the background.

We wanted to stay at the Royal Scots Hotel again because we had enjoyed it so much the first time. Lauren wanted more souvenirs, so we headed out to High Street again and walked the golden mile. Lauren picked up some wool sweaters and cotton T-shirts.

We decided to spend the second week of our vacation in the Channel Islands. We took the train back to London and made arrangements to fly to St. Peter Port on Guernsey Island. We took off from Heathrow the following morning and landed on the island. We took a cab to the biggest hotel on the island and unpacked our luggage in our room. For the first time on our trip, we took a nap to gather our strength.

The English Channel warms the Channel Islands all year long, and even though it was late September, flowers were everywhere in bloom. We explored St. Peter Port that night, weaving in and out of quaint little side streets. After dinner at a cozy restaurant, we headed down to the marina. Looking back at the town was a beautiful sight. Despite our nap, we were tired and decided to call it a day. We went to sleep that night amidst the warm waters of the English Channel.

There was only one historical attraction on Guernsey Island, and that was King John's Castle built in 1215. This was the same King John who signed the Magna Carta, and the castle has remained relatively unchanged since 1215. Lauren and I took a cab out to the castle and booked a tour. Inside, the suits of armor were polished and showed what the knights wore during the Middle Ages.

After touring the castle, we decided to take a walking tour of the island. Guernsey Island is only twenty-six miles in circumference, and we decided to start on the north coast. The water in the coves was aquamarine, which surprised us. We didn't expect to see Caribbean-colored water in the English Channel.

The architecture and culture were a curious blend of British and French. Even though the islands were eighty miles from the coast of Britain and only ten miles from the coast of France, they belonged to Britain.

Most of the natives make their living fishing the waters of the English Channel. The rest made their living through tourism. The islands had their own currency and their own postage stamps. I collected samples of both as souvenirs.

The only other must-see in the islands besides King John's Castle is the Jersey Zoo on Jersey Island. The naturalist Gerald Durrell collected animals in danger of becoming extinct and brought them to his zoo on Jersey Island. Countless species have been saved from extinction thanks to his efforts. Lauren and I took the ferry to Jersey Island and spent our entire third day there. Before leaving, we made an anonymous donation to the zoo.

In many ways, Guernsey Island reminded me of Bermuda. The water was roughly the same color and the flowers, especially the bougainvillea, were everywhere. We really had seen the main attractions of the islands in three days, and we decided we wanted to spend the last two days of our vacation back in London. We packed our bags at the St. Pierre Park Hotel and made arrangements to spend our last two days in London at the Allison House Hotel.

As our plane took off the next day, we took pictures of King John's Castle from the air. We couldn't wait to get our pictures developed to see if we had captured its essence.

Back in London, we were starting to get a little homesick. We wondered how Mochi was doing at the Westchester Kennel Club. Lauren was tempted to call them, but I dissuaded her from it. Lauren became increasingly worried about Mochi to the point where we decided to make our vacation a day short. We changed our airline tickets for tomorrow and looked forward to getting home. After such a long break, I was actually anxious to get back to work. I had to write a synopsis of the conference, and I started it on the plane. I didn't want Dr. Margolis to think I had all fun and no work.

When we arrived at JFK at around eight p.m., we hoped that Mochi hadn't picked up kennel cough. We arrived at our home by nine p.m. and we started unpacking everything. We both still had one more day off to enjoy, and our only chore was that we had to pick up Mochi. We both enjoyed the thought of having one more day off before going back to work.

CHAPTER

Mochi had contracted kennel cough. Our first day back, we had to take Mochi to the vet. He prescribed some medication that we hoped would work and then we went home.

We still hadn't finished unpacking from our trip, so we started in on it as soon as we got home. After an hour, we had put everything away and we started focusing on what needed to be accomplished before going back to work.

I was devising strategies to avoid Mary at work, and Lauren was thinking about her Mergers and Acquisitions class. I definitely thought Mary deserved a rebuking, but I didn't want to do it in front of Dr. Margolis. Lauren knew something was on my mind, but I decided to never tell her about the Mary episode.

Before we jumped back into the rat race, we called our parents and told them we were home safe. They were relieved to hear from us, and we told them we had the time of our lives.

By seven a.m. the next morning, we were back in a New York state of mind. I was back on my train to Manhattan and so was Lauren. As usual, I got off at Grand Central Station and started walking towards Phitzer's office building at forty-second and Third Avenue. I made my way through the throngs of people coming out of Grand central, and I knew I was going to suffer from the post-vacation blues.

Dr. Margolis wanted a trip report within a week. Fortunately, I had taken copious notes during the conference and that shouldn't be a problem. It was my mental state that I was more worried about. I didn't know how to combat the post-vacation blues. I kept thinking about what a wonderful time I had, but for some reason, it just didn't cheer me up. I passed Mary in a hallway and I just avoided her. I didn't feel like confronting her just yet.

I kept my head low all day, barely looking up from my work to face the world. What was going on? I had never felt like this before after a vacation.

When I got home, Lauren noticed my mood and asked what was wrong. I couldn't give her a one hundred percent accurate answer. I just said "post-vacation blues." She told me to go fix it. I didn't feel like it and went to bed early.

Slowly but surely over the next few weeks, I was able to discern the source of my depression. It had to do with the fact that I was actually tempted by Mary's offer in London. I had fooled myself into thinking that I wasn't tempted, but I knew that deep down inside I really was. It made me realize that Lauren's and my love for each other was only as strong as we made it. We were human beings with frailties and imperfections and we were going to stumble and fall. We were both going to be tempted by other people, and I had barely passed the Mary test.

I wondered what man would come along who would tempt Lauren. Would it be in the near future or the distant future? Would he be better looking than me? Inevitably, the day would come, and I realized that was the source of my depression, that Lauren's and my marriage may not be able to overcome all obstacles. There were millions of reasons why the divorce rate was more than fifty percent. Which one would do us in? Even the love for our child— Mochi—may not be able to overcome the forces working against us. Then again, maybe we would.

CHAPTER

The seed of doubt had been planted and it was spreading like a wild vine throughout my consciousness. Lauren noticed the difference in me and she didn't like it. Unfortunately, I wasn't able to turn it off.

New York was such a jungle, such a cacophony of stresses and noises that I knew my nervous system couldn't go on indefinitely. I was a small town boy from rural Pennsylvania, not a corporate mogul born into wealth. I longed for the peaceful, halcyon days in Philadelphia.

I didn't like getting swallowed into the masses every day, trying to distinguish myself from the eight million other worker bees who swarmed into Manhattan every day. That artistic streak in me was creating a pocket of rebellion in my soul, and sooner or later that streak would demand its freedom. In my spare time, I started writing poetry, and one of my first poems was this little ditty:

Business 5.0

It all started in Manahatta about four hundred years ago
When the local Indians accepted a bribe
From Peter Minuit to the tune of twenty-four dollars
They didn't know that after that, they would have to run and
hide.

For twenty-four dollars' worth of wampum
They sold their tribal lands
The rest they say is history
Not knowing they had been shammed.

Now corporations in tall buildings
Buy and sell millions every day
The nicest places to live in the world
Are in Westchester County by Long Island Bay.

Now about eight million people live around and in
Manhattan
And fortunes come and go
We live in a Brave New World
Of Business 5.0.

I do not know why I thought New York was in its fifth generation of business—poetic license I guess. I just knew it rang true. All I knew was that the poetry was keeping my depression in check and placating my artistic streak. I looked forward to writing some new poetry every week.

It was unfortunate that my artistic streak was blooming in New York City of all places. New York had a great art scene—for the already rich. Lauren and I were at the bottom of the totem pole in that category. Saving was just so damn hard in New York. As we struggled to pay our mortgage and make ends meet, Lauren started to resent my artistic streak more and more. Of course, I didn't make matters any easier because all I wanted to do when I got home was write poetry. I liked walking the dog too.

In the meantime, Lauren was taking night classes to finish her MBA. She started criticizing me for not cleaning to her satisfaction and I resented it. I did the best job I knew how, and if it wasn't good enough, so be it. Lauren's frustration with me grew as my artistic streak grew. The tension of this created unpleasantness, and the unpleasantness grew into dissatisfaction.

One day Lauren came home and said she wanted us to go to a marriage counselor. I reluctantly agreed. At our first appointment, Lauren unleashed on me, telling the therapist that I was a lousy cleaner who had an artistic streak a mile wide. I countered by saying that my artistic streak provided me an outlet that I desperately needed in a very stressful world.

Worse yet, we were starting to lose our physical attraction to each other. I was cuddling with Mochi more than with my wife at night. The little furball would make a pillow around my head and stay that way all night. Lauren, on the other hand, stayed on her side of the bed and didn't touch me.

In short, our marriage was in trouble, and oblivious me, all I wanted to do to soothe my soul was write poetry. I had visions of me giving up my job at Phitzer and becoming a Mad Manhattan poet. Thank God I had never told Lauren of this wild dream or we'd probably already be divorced.

I managed to keep my artistic streak at bay all day at work, and then at night at home, I would unleash a torrent of poetry. I must have looked like a man possessed, with crumpled sheets of paper all over the floor and my pen flying across the page. My hand was a flying dervish wielding a fountain pen.

CHAPTER

After several months of therapy, Lauren and I realized that we weren't making any progress. I couldn't change—I was already too fixed in my ways. Furthermore, I didn't want to change—I liked who I was, and if that didn't make Lauren happy she could divorce me.

In the fall, Lauren came home one day, and something was different. There was a calm assurance about her that made me uncomfortable.

"Do you want a divorce?" Lauren asked. "Only if you do," I replied.

"I think we are fundamentally incompatible, and I think we should get a divorce," she said.

"O.K., if that's what you want," I said. "I'm moving out this weekend," she said.

It was settled. My marriage was over. I walked into the study to write poetry. When we met, Lauren was the best thing that ever happened to me, and now she hated my guts. I wasn't that crazy about her anymore either.

When the movers came that weekend, I tried to stay out of the way. Most of the good furniture belonged to Lauren and I hated to see it go, but I knew it wasn't mine. I decided to get out of the house. I drove to our favorite diner and ordered a meal.

* * *

A few weeks later, I found out that Lauren was dating someone from her office. She was evasive, of course, but I did find out his name—Chris. I always hated the name Chris because it was a derivative of Christ, and I knew that no one on this planet except Christ was perfect.

While our house was on the market, I continued to write poetry. It was the only thing that relieved my soul. I also had to find a new place to live. I found an apartment nearby and put a security deposit on it. Since Lauren was gone, the sooner I got out of the house the better. After living in a comfortable home, it was difficult adjusting to apartment living again. I was used to the space of a home, and I also missed my jungle of a backyard. I also missed consistent sex. Dating after a divorce is never as much fun as dating for the never married. I became philosophical in my attitude towards women. I wouldn't overextend my heartstrings again. I had learned my lesson. At least now I could pursue my artistic passions unfettered.

My job at Phitzer no longer seemed so important. I didn't have the credentials to make Vice President, and perhaps Lauren saw that. I was just working to survive, but it certainly wasn't what I was living for. I had the soul of an artist, and only through art would I be able to find fulfillment.

My apartment in New Rochelle was sufficient, but it did not inspire me to write. I missed my study in the Cape Cod. It's amazing how sensitive artists are to their environment. I couldn't find inspiration within the four walls of my apartment so I went to the public library to write. I became a fixture in the New Rochelle Public Library.

I performed my duties at Phitzer with no enthusiasm and came home and pursued my real passion. I experienced a new world of emptiness that I had never experienced before. I was becoming ever more numb because the harshness of reality pushed me towards emotional numbness, and yet I knew this harshness was necessary to force my hand as an artist. It was a paradox.

CHAPTER

I was good at putting up a good front. Dr. Margolis noticed a shift in my demeanor, but my work standard remained the same and he didn't say anything. I showed up, did my job, and then went home.

At night my heart came alive. Sitting in a remote section of the New Rochelle Public Library, I felt inspired by all the books. I couldn't help it; I started thinking about the early days of my marriage. I felt a poem coming on, and here it was:

Marriage

John Donne once said
I am every dead thing
In whom love wrought new alchemy:
And so it was with me
A soldier who had seen
At least fifty ways to die
Resurrected by the sight of her
Being so lucky to survive
And yet my luck did not end there
Because it was as though God granted me one last wish
And behold, it came true when she said yes.

And on that day, time stood still
If only for an instant
And while flesh to flesh and blood to blood
And bone to bone were blessed as one
So were my guardian angel and her guardian angel
And we knew that we would be an invincible team
And Heaven opened up before the altar
And for a few moments
The witnesses could see its glory
All heads bowed down in its presence
And then time started again, with a new clock.

My poetry informed me that I would now know loneliness without Lauren. I had always considered myself somewhat of an outsider and I didn't expect loneliness to affect me too much, but after living with someone for years and then not having that person be there for you is a much more severe test. My stomach muscles were learning a new meaning of emptiness.

After a few months, I realized that there was no point in trying to "keep up appearances." My apartment sucked, and I wasn't sure if I would ever have the money to buy a really nice home again. All my possessions I could squeeze into a one-bedroom apartment and that amazed me. Also, I got stuck with the Civic station wagon, not the Prelude. It was a low-end car that I would have to do something about once I had the money.

I realized that my artistic streak had put me on the road to down and out hood. Instead of a secure future, I now had a future of uncertainty. Given that I was not heir to a fortune, I would have to sink or swim all on my own.

That was the concept that scared me the most—self-determination. I had always heard the expression "self-made man" and wondered what it really meant; now I was about to find out.

Being trained as a biologist, I thought a lot about animals. I had studied the courtship rituals of many species. For example, I was fascinated with the courtship ritual of bald eagles. To impress the female, the male bald eagle soars high into the air and performs acrobatic stunts. If the female bald eagle is impressed, she takes off after him and tries to duplicate his stunts. To mate, the male bald eagle flies underneath the female and then turns upside down. They lock talons, and while the male is impregnating the female, they do a free fall in the air. After the act is complete, they disengage before falling to their deaths. With such a difficult act required to perpetuate the species, it's a miracle they are not yet extinct.

With such obstacles to overcome, I looked back with pride in how I had captured Lauren's heart. Perhaps I hadn't been as daring as a bald eagle, but I had flown her to the most romantic city in the world and spread my feathers, and at that moment in time it was enough. I had shown the true colors of my feathers, and they were hues of blue, green, and purple. They were the cool colors, and I was cool and self-assured. Mine were the colors of the violet-bellied hummingbird, and as I started thinking about hummingbirds, this poem came to me:

The Kiss of the Hummingbird

Flitter—that's what hummingbirds do
Stationary—in midair—hovering
Their wings a blur whose distinct features
Can only be seen by slow-motion photography.

At feeders filled with sucrose nectar
They dip their long beaks into the reservoir
Remaining still in space—
The blur that is their wings doing their job.

Sometimes I wonder how they can absorb
So much energy from the nectar
To keep their wings beating the way they do –
How is this possible?

And what about love amongst the hummingbirds?
Do the males court the females?
And if they are successful, do they kiss?
With three-inch long beaks for lips—do they kiss?

My guess is that instead of kissing
To show affection, they align their beaks
And just let the ends touch while feeding
Perhaps this is what nature intended kissing to be.

Antelope and moose touch noses
Whales and seals touch fins
Humans, as far as I know, are the only species
Whose lips have become erogenous zones.

Perhaps we could learn something from the hummingbirds
And learn to use positional geometry to show affection
I'm sure that once we gain our wings
We'll act more like hummingbirds.

One phrase of the poem stuck in my mind—once we gain our wings. I started thinking—do angels really have wings? Of course, they do! Every mention of angels in the Bible describes them as having wings. Perhaps birds are a more highly evolved species than we are.

I was metaphysical. I still like Plato's down-to-earth definition of man—a featherless biped. He got it right— we are only skin, blood, muscle, and bone, and when the hormones of love wear off they are gone forever. The chemical reaction is unidirectional: there is no going back. Some couples manage to navigate these chemical changes over a lifetime, but most do not. I was in the majority with those who couldn't handle the changes.

CHAPTER

As the realities of living in New York impinged on my consciousness, I realized that I had better develop a plan. I think it was more that than anything that did me in with Lauren—no plan. She evidently had bigger plans than I did. She wasn't content to be married to a lowto mid-level pharmaceutical employee. She felt she deserved better.

Each day I performed my job quietly and then I took the train home. Each day on the train I played a little game with myself—count the Jews. I counted each person in my car who I thought was a Jew. Of course, I had no way of knowing if I was close or not—I only went by looks. There are Jews who don't look like Jews and there are non-Jews who look like Jews. A hundred years ago, Jacob Riis called New York Jewtown, so I started calling New York Jewtown.

Of course, not all rich New Yorkers are Jews. Gentiles lived around me in Westchester County or in Connecticut. In Westchester County and Greenwich, Connecticut everyone drove beamers or Mercedes, wore expensive clothes, and took fancy vacations. The neighborhoods were full of trophy wives in big houses. I thought about the movie The Stepford Wives and thought about how much truth there was in that fictional tale. Not just the women, though, but the men as well kind of acted like robots. The men were expected to have high-powered Wall Street jobs and the women were expected to be beautiful. That was not just the stereotype but the true reality.

Of course, not everybody in Westchester County was plastic. There were artists and painters like me, although we were a distinct minority. There were some mad Manhattan poets who were for the most part homeless and thus down and out. And there were guys like me, who pretended to fit in but who really didn't.

One thing New York forces you to do is, to be honest with yourself. I realized that I was not a superachiever, just a smart man with an artistic streak. I was playing the game, but my heart was no longer in it. I was going through the motions—showing up at work and doing my job—and some say that would no longer be enough. I would have to make a value-added contribution just to keep any job. I wasn't there yet, but that's where I was headed.

At work, I was put on a new product to treat erectile dysfunction. My job was to make sure that the data was clean and that all the i's were dotted and the t's crossed on all documentation. My colleagues called me Mr. Clean. It wasn't a particularly difficult job, just tedious and repetitive. Nevertheless, I performed it to the best of my ability and that was good enough for me to keep my job.

One of the great things about working in Manhattan is that during breaks and at lunchtime there are innumerable diversions with which to entertain oneself. So even though my job was tedious, I could walk outside at break time and take my mind off my job for a few minutes.

One day at lunchtime I walked the few blocks to Times Square and studied the hookers. They were the lowest class of prostitutes—the streetwalkers. The smart hookers became call girls. Looking at the hookers on Times Square, I couldn't help but notice the analogy between hookers and anybody who worked for money. In a sense, we all prostituted ourselves for money. You give your body and your mind to a company for a certain wage and then you go home and try to enjoy life. We are all prostitutes to a certain degree.

With that thought in mind, I walked back to my office. I sat there for a while, and then it came to me what my artistic streak was all about. Poetry set me free! When I wrote poetry, I felt like I was free. And at that moment, I felt like being free in my office. I composed this poem about the little blue pill I was working on:

Viagra Pours Like Niagara Falls

In these bustling days of stress and economic worry
There came to be a little blue pill
And even though they made it in a hurry
Man alive did it ever sell.

Now men over the age of forty-five
Can have their penis come alive
As though they were just reaching puberty
Their erections now stand as tall and proud as the Statue of
Liberty.

The sales of the little blue pill have gone into the billions
And the men whose lives it has changed is now in the millions
The sales of Viagra pour like Niagara Falls
And men past their prime stand proud and tall.

Oh how wonderful the miracles of modern chemistry
So what if a few men die attempting to regain their virility
So what if this pony only has one good trick
Men who would have been lonely now have one stiff prick.

On this day, I hadn't been caught writing poetry in my office, but I knew the day would come when I would. It was only a matter of time. And when that day came, I would lose my job, and when I lost my job I would become down and out. Maybe that's what scared Lauren about my artistic streak—the fact that one day it would lead me to down and out hood. She was right to leave me. I saw it all so clearly now.

CHAPTER

I took the train each day to work, one face among the vast masses of faces who commuted into Manhattan each day. The only difference now is that now I no longer had another face to come home to. All I could do was look in the mirror. I realized how empty my existence would become without friends and poetry. And then I thought what a shame it was that Lauren and I did not have a family. Perhaps that was part of God's plan, I do not know, but I started to feel a vast emptiness in my life without her.

As I walked on Forty-Second Street on my way to work, one day I noticed a fertility clinic a few blocks from my office. I stopped in one day and found out they paid thirty bucks a pop for sperm. I figured why not make money and save my sperm for posterity at the same time? At this point, I figured it was unlikely that I'd ever have children, so why not preserve my seed just in case some woman in the future liked me. That way, in some indirect way, my genes may one day continue to flourish on this earth. After I made my first deposit, I walked back to my office and wrote this poem about the experience:

Sperm Bank

O little sperm contained in glass

Thank God you weren't taken from my ass

But instead, from a cup

After reading Hustler, which got me up.

Who knows what people you will become

When your lives outside the glass have begun

Perhaps there is an Aristotle among you

Or perhaps an ass like Spiro Agnew.

My little seed may populate the planet

After the world has become a ball of granite

And perhaps we will never again know

A Mom and Dad who love to watch their kids grow.

If nothing else, this little ditty cheered me up. So what if I wasn't good enough for Lauren. Some women in the near or distant future would appreciate my merits and want to carry my seed to term.

In the meantime, this was New York, and the daily pursuit was money. Each day, I put my thinking cap on and pretended to be a superbrain to fit in with the other superbrains at Phitzer. I did not want to go back to publishing wages, because that would lead to down and out hood. I had suffered enough by losing Lauren; I didn't feel like climbing down the socioeconomic ladder as well. Deep in my heart, I knew that was where I was headed because of my artistic streak, but I didn't feel like going there just yet. I wanted to postpone my downfall as long as possible. Hence, I performed my job to my utmost ability and kept a stiff upper lip, just like a good Englishman is supposed to.

The other element I had to fight besides poverty was insanity. Now that I was alone again, I noticed that my usually keen mind was beginning to ramble. At times, I rambled extensively. When I had Lauren in my life, my mind was honed and focused. Now, without her, my mind took long philosophical vacations, but still, I was able to function in the real world. However, the seed was planted within me that perhaps I would no longer be able to function in the real world.

A hundred years ago, during Jacob Riis' time, insane men were sent to Ward Island, and insane women were sent to Blackwell Island. Jacob Riis had noticed the correlation between poverty and insanity and so had George Orwell forty years later, and fortunately, I had read both of them. I knew that if I ever got bumped down from pharmaceutical wages to publishing wages it would eventually wind up in the new Ward Island—Bellevue Hospital.

The other possibility, of course, was that I would meet and fall in love with another woman who would bring me back to physical and mental health. There was always hope that this would happen.

Over the next several months, I began to notice that it was hard to live in New York even on a mid-level pharmaceutical employee's salary. My apartment was small, but it was all I could afford. I wasn't expecting a raise for at least another year, and I knew that I didn't have the energy to take a second job at night. Slowly I began to realize that maybe New York was too competitive for me. I longed for the more placid atmosphere of Philadelphia. Homes were less expensive there, and the people didn't have quite as hard an edge. I let my brain ramble about moving back to Philadelphia.

I started going to poetry readings at night after work. I thought perhaps that if I immersed myself with kindred spirits that it would ease my pain. One night at a poetry reading I met Yorick Alfresco. He was wearing a funky Walt Whitmanesque hat and he chain-smoked Marlboros. After hearing him read and talking to him for a while, I realized that, just like Shakespeare's Yorick in Hamlet, he was a clown. He was an ex-druggie who had blown out his brain an acid-turned artist. If his poetry hadn't been so bad, I may have wanted to befriend him. But his poetry was all over the place, it didn't rhyme, and there was no message

I could discern. He had high entertainment value, however, so I decided to be at least congenial with him.

I missed Mochi tremendously, and I started visiting the local dog shelter with the hopes of finding one that I could bond with. One day, there was a new Lhasaapso at the shelter. He was gray and white, with tufts of white sticking out of his gray head. When I looked at him, I could have sworn that he smiled back at me. I asked the keeper to take him out of his pen. When he did, he ran up to me and wanted to be petted. At that moment, it was over. The decision had been made—I wanted him. I paid the keeper two hundred dollars and took the Lhasaapso home with me.

I stopped going to poetry readings for a few weeks to bond with my animal and to learn how to take care of him. I fed him once in the morning before going to work and once in the evening when I got home. I walked him every morning and he loved sleeping with me. I decided to name him Sam. After a few weeks, we had our routine down, and I felt comfortable leaving him alone. I started going to poetry readings again. One evening, I read this poem that I had written about Sam:

Canine Companion

And so I stroke your fleece white coat
And give you proper grooming
You are my Tibetan guard dog
And I always give you good combing.

I march you out to walk each morn
Your nose leads you where you need to smell
The other dogs in the neighborhoods pee
You lead me on as if in a spell.

You once protected the monks of ancient Tibet
For centuries from the samurai
O loyal Lhasa, you are the best of pets
And now I understand why

You could only be given as gifts to the priests
You were not to be bought or sold
You were their little furry companions
And with mine alone, I will grow old.

And then I think it's kind of sad
That in fifty years of hard living
The only true friend I ever had
Was a dog.

And now I knew why dogs were thought of as man's best friend. They not only appreciate every little thing you do for them, they are also eternally loyal. We do not live in a dog-eat-dog world, but a human-eat-human world. Dogs don't eat each other, people do.

Another advantage of having a dog is that it tends to keep one grounded. A dog needs to be fed twice a day, walked at least once a day, and bathed and groomed at least once a month. There are visits to the vet when your pet gets sick, and your dog should have a license. In short, it is a lot like having a baby. If you can stretch your imagination, a man and his dog are a family.

CHAPTER

Since I had a lot of free time on my hands, I reread Jacob Riis' How The Other Half Lives. His perceptions were as true today as they were a hundred years ago. I particularly liked the line in the chapter The Bohemians, "lives, like clothes, are worn through and out before being put aside." I thought about that line, and I realized that I was only a paycheck away from poverty. If I ever lost my job at Phitzer, I'd be out on the streets within a couple of months. There was no "portfolio" in my family—no "nest egg." In other words, I was not from a wealthy family. I had no security blanket, no safety net. I was walking on a high trapeze line, and if I fell I would be down and out for good.

At work, I kept my head buried in my work and did not dare make any waves. I understood the precariousness of my situation and knew that I had to keep a low profile. I had to make Dr. Margolis happy in any way that I could. I learned what his buttons were and how not to push them.

I did not dare to write any more poetry at work. I realized the importance of leaving the heavy thinking at home.

At home, I would reflect upon what I had seen that day. I realized that there were millions of people in New York who were in the same precarious situation I was in. For the most part, that was why they were in New York—to make enough money to feed their families. I realized that my position wasn't that bad—all I had to do was feed myself and my dog. What about the people with five kids who didn't have a huge portfolio? What if they lost their job?

With these thoughts in mind, I felt another poem ready to emerge. I cleared my mind, and this is what came to me:

A Perverted Landscape

Back in the day when the pioneers headed west,
There was a spirit of cooperation.
They relied on one another for survival.
What happened?

Now that the West has been conquered
It's every man for himself. Sink or swim.
Make money or die.
Oh, what a perverted landscape.

Do you think that Washington and Jefferson
Envisioned such a free-for-all?

Now every man and woman, regardless of race, color, or creed
can vote.
So what. It's all based on greed.
Politicians suckle their constituents like sugar daddies,
And sprinkle pork wherever they can throughout their district.

What we have now is a no man's land.
An interruption in the battlefield.
There are no more safe havens.
Pay or hit the streets.
Oh, what a perverted landscape.
That's all it is.

I realized that was why I was a Democrat—I cared about everybody, not just the elite. My parents had raised me that way. Lauren had been raised as a Republican. I guess that was the fundamental difference between us— she was an elitist and I was not. And in the end, that is what drove us apart.

Max and Rick, my best friends, were now not within easy commuting distance. As a consequence, I started spending more time with Yorick. It was a shame; Yorick had a good heart, but he had destroyed his mind with drugs. Consequently, he couldn't hold a job and was perpetually poor. I'd constantly be loaning him fives and tens that he'd never pay back. After a few months, I was getting tired of being his benefactor—I had my own financial constraints. Maybe if I had an ounce of respect for his poetry, I'd feel differently.

I was slugging it out in Manhattan every day, and he was still living in his Mommy's house. Even though he was somebody to go to poetry readings with, I knew early on that he could never become a real friend like Max or Rick. He was only somebody who I could just barely tolerate.

At work, I realized that my resentment towards Yorick was building up. I was cleaning data all day for a major pharmaceutical company, while Yorick was sitting in a coffee shop all day smoking Marlboros. Finally, at work one day, while I was thinking about Yorick, a single word came to my mind—useless. I knew that I had to write a poem with that title. I waited until I got home from work that day and this is what I came up with:

Useless

Sometimes they are called by different names
Like backsliders or slackers
There will always be different names to describe them
Because no matter which profession they choose
They will always be hackers.

I'm glad I don't count the useless among my friends
They certainly aren't a good example and they don't make
amends.
I'm glad not too many make it to doctor
Or someone on whom one's life depends
Because the useless usually end up bonkers.

There's no need to point
They know who they are
They wanted to make it through this life
Without any battle scars
Their raison d'etre never unfurls.

There are not many success stories among the useless
They drift through life without a cause
And when their time is done
And they have to give an account of themselves
They see that if they had tried, they would have won.

There's a difference between those who are clueless
And those who are useless;
Those who are clueless just don't get it
While those who are useless usually get it but don't do it It
is their nature to backslide and tell the hard workers to cram it.

Instead, they cheat on their spouses, they cheat on exams,
They watch the go-getters bustin their ass while they work
on their tans,
And when people get sick of them and call them to task
They disappear with an Alakazam
When all they had to do to be successful was ask.

Without really trying they make up good lies
And tell their spouses and neighbors next year they'll try
But they never do, and when they end up old, alone, and
toothless
And they're asked what they did with their lives
They look dumbfounded and say "I—I guess I was useless."

I knew I would never read this poem in the company
of Yorick. He would have known immediately that the
shoe fit. I didn't want to disgrace him to his face, but
behind his back. I guess living in New York and losing a
wife, I had developed a bit of a mean streak after all.

CHAPTER

I had been to London and Paris, and even though they were huge cities, there was a sense of comfort one had while visiting there. Unlike London and Paris, there was a harshness to New York that is almost indescribable. The American capital of commerce was a greed mongers paradise, but not much else. Compared to its city's size, Central Park is a joke.

New York had demons that could only exist in New York. Hell's Kitchen got its name for a reason. They say that if you can make it in New York you can make it anywhere. Maybe that's true, but for everyone who makes it, there are a hundred who don't. New York is more often a dream breaker than a dream maker. I was one of those whose dreams had been broken in New York. This is where my marriage failed, and where I was now living alone without friends. All I had was my job, and I didn't have the education to move up the ladder. I was stuck, just barely surviving in a hostile world.

If dreams shape reality, New York is a nightmare. The dreams that shaped London and Paris resulted in beauty. The dreams that shaped New York produced a monstrosity. What dream produced Harlem, or the junkyard called Staten Island? Perhaps New York was God's revenge on Americans for being too greedy. I don't know, but I started thinking more and more about dreams to the point where I wrote a poem about them, and here it is:

Two Hundred and Fifty Thousand Dreams

As babies we begin to dream
We turn in our cribs, eyes shut
Moving to the rhythms of our inner images
Under our lids, our eyes pulse and flutter

And the years go by, and we grow
And as we get bigger
Our dreams get longer and more vivid
Until when we are fully grown
Our dreams have also reached their full stature

At the apex of our dreams
We achieve unity with the unconscious world
The collective unconscious where all things are connected
And people go through their waking hours
Following the impulses of that collective unconscious

So many dreams, and alternate realities
So many dreamers, moving to the collective pulse
Of the unconscious world.
There are approximately two hundred and fifty million
dreamers in this country
If we all dream a quarter of a million dreams in a lifetime
That makes for a total of approximately sixty-two trillion
dreams
And of these, how many are true?
How many are true?

There it is. It ends with a question mark due to the intangible nature of dreams. In my opinion, the dreams that created New York produced hell, not heaven. Perhaps I wasn't greedy enough to appreciate it for what it was—a corporate jungle. I'd prefer the Amazon rainforest jungle any day of the week.

Madmen, poets, and philosophers all inhabited New York. However, so did pit bull stock traders, shark investment bankers, and gay publishing house executives. It was the ultimate melting pot, which is really what America is all about. Unfortunately, there is no safety net in New York. Prices in New York become increasingly unreasonable every year, and only those who are lucky in life can keep up. Although I had a good job at Phitzer, I could feel myself sinking. Ever since I had lost Lauren, my sense of economic security had been diminished. There was a Main Line girl who wanted big things, who was probably going to inherit a lot of money someday. Had I been able to stay on that train, I perhaps would have been wealthy one day. Instead, I was on the oblivion express. Not only had I suffered economically, but in addition, I knew deep down that my self-confidence with women had suffered. In a sense, I had suffered a double whammy. If it weren't for that damned artistic streak of mine, I would have been sitting pretty in a few years. I realized that I hadn't played my cards very well with Lauren. To keep a super achieving woman happy, you had to be able to bend and flex, and I wasn't very good at that. My personality and temperament were not conducive to being told what to do. I was a free spirit, a maverick, and I didn't always play by the rules. Most artists are not necessarily straight shooters, and I was no exception. The casualty of this temperament was my marriage— lesson learned. At least I was free to pursue other opportunities.

And New York was full of opportunities. Diversions were everywhere if one cared to pursue them. The problem was, I didn't feel self-confident enough to pursue them. I had a mid-level job in a pharmaceutical company, and I could barely afford my rent and to feed my dog and me. I had no real friends to speak of here, and I missed Philadelphia. I was starting to think what the hell, why not totally give myself over to my artistic side and see where it led me? At night I started going out to local bars to observe the local color. Most of the customers were habitués with one sorry story or another, and for the most part, I didn't like any of them. Half of them were alcoholics, boozing it up to escape their pain; only the young patrons seemed to be truly enjoying themselves.

One night, I decided to try to get Lauren off my mind with an alcoholic blitz assault. I would drink until I could no longer remember her name. I didn't want to do this anywhere close to my home where someone might know me, but in some part of the city, I was unfamiliar with. I had never really been to the upper west side of Manhattan, so I hopped on a train headed in that general direction. I got off the train. I knew that it wouldn't be that hard to find a bar because there are ten bars for every church in Manhattan. I found one and walked in. I sat down and ordered a vodka martini with a beer chaser. I thought that mixing the hard stuff with the soft stuff would get me drunk faster. In a half hour, I downed four martinis and beers, and I was just getting started. I knew I was almost drunk, but I could still remember Lauren's name, so I knew I still had a ways to go. The funny thing about alcohol is that it erases short-term memory but leaves long-term memory alone. So even though my short-term memory was going, there was nothing I could do about my long-term memory, which included Lauren. I couldn't remember how I had gotten to this bar, or even where I was. I was just sober enough to keep ordering drinks.

The next day, I woke up in my bed with a pounding headache. I couldn't remember how I had gotten home. Fortunately, it was Saturday morning and I didn't have to go to work. My artistic streak wouldn't be satisfied until I had written a poem about last night's experience. I walked to my medicine chest, grabbed five aspirin and popped them in, and then sat down to put pen to paper. Here is what I came up with:

Finding the Wizard

I thought Oz was a real city
Until I came here
And saw that the streets weren't paved with gold

So I went into a bar
And ordered some beer . . . liquid gold
And got loaded on my ass

A drunken poet,
Pleading with the Muse of Alcohol
For further intoxication in her spirit

"O Holy Ale! Loose this numb tongue
To make sober speech to that woman"
But that ungrateful bitch just sprinkled laughter
In the mouths of the habitués

So I stumbled out the door
Onto the sidewalk
And laid my head on the curb to sleep
But in my eyes of night
I didn't see tin man,
Or cowardly lion,
Or scarecrow

Instead I saw Frankenstein
And Werewolf
And myself strewn up on a lamppost
Where my night body got ripped to pieces

So I carried the carcass of my dreams
Back to the sacred cave
Where my memories are stored
To patch back the images of Oz

I came to in a jail cell
And saw a cop come unlock the door
And say "Get the hell outta here, and don't let it happen again."

So I got up and started walking
Walking through Oz
And then I remembered something, something about beer
Oh yea, it was last night's great accomplishment . . . I thought

Poetry and alcohol accomplish the same ends
They both make life seem better

But I knew that wasn't right
So I tried to think of something better
And then I thought. . . .

They are both like taking a bus ride
To the far side of the city
And getting off empty inside
That sounded more like it—Christ, it even rhymed
So I decided to try it, just to see

I rolled through the city
And found that it was true
Because when I got off, I wondered what I was doing there

I was lost, and afraid
And the streets weren't paved with gold
And there weren't any good fairies to take me home

And then I knew, man, what a fool
I came all the way from nowhere
Just to wash my feet
In the rainbows of the street.

It was so convoluted, I knew it would take years for me to understand this poem. Still, I was proud of it—I knew it was a good poem. It truly explored my artistic side—the source of my downfall.

CHAPTER

36

By late Saturday afternoon, my headache had subsided, but I felt like I was becoming Yorick. What a stupid stunt I had pulled! There was no good reason for it. I had achieved nothing other than a poem. Big deal.

I called Max to see if he wanted to get together with me tonight. He said it would be O.K. to stay overnight. There was a party he was going to, and he said I could come.

I was very excited to visit with Max. I hadn't seen him for several months, and I was especially excited to be getting out of New York. I took the northern route around the city and then down Route 81. I was there in two hours. He showed me in, and I put my overnight bag on the floor.

At the party were a number of good-looking women. I approached one and found out her name was Lynn. Lynn was a beautiful brunette who had blue eyes, just like

Lauren. I told her I lived in New York and she seemed to be impressed with that. When she asked me where and I said Now Rochelle, she seemed a little less impressed. I looked across the room and saw that Max had engaged a redhead in conversation. I asked Lynn for her phone number and she gave it to me. Max looked like he was successful in getting a number too, and then he walked over to me and said, "Looks like you're on the comeback trail."

"Her name is Karen, and she's an attorney in the district attorney's office," I replied.

"The one I was talking to—her name is Cheryl," he said. "She works for an insurance company."

Having both been successful in obtaining numbers, we decided to split the party and go to a popular singles bar named Buddha. There was a giant red Buddha sitting in the middle of the room, and there were gorgeous girls everywhere. I loved to watch Max hunt. His appetite was insatiable. He had just gotten a phone number, and now he wanted more. I watched as his eagle eyes surveyed the room picking out the "targets" he was interested in. Once he had identified his optimal target, his tongue was quick with the right words. Nine times out of ten it became only a pleasant conversation, but one in ten times there really was some interest. Being a sociologist, Max knew that finding love was a numbers game. No at-bats, no hits. What made him truly unique was his ability to pursue women with unflagging devotion to his creed— never give up, and never shy away from an attempt to get to know someone.

I really admired that about Max. Living according to his creed was what Max was all about. Perhaps that was the difference between me and Max; Max was true to his creed, while I was not. I was living a lie. By nature and temperament I was an artist, and yet here I was working in the corporate kingdom of New York. Of course, I knew I was doing it out of fear and economic necessity. I didn't like to starve any more than the next person. But deep down, I knew the charade couldn't go on forever. Someday, I would have to be true to my calling and give up the corporate world and either go into academia or become a writer. I knew it was fear that tightened my sphincter tone to survive in the corporate world. I had seen down and out from a distance, and I had no desire to get any closer. Even with my job, I could feel it breathing down my neck and I didn't know what to do about it. I slept on Max's couch that night knowing that my predicament was real. Max was still in graduate school and hadn't really faced the real world yet. He was still cocky and self-assured when it came to women. I was still cocky but not so self-assured.

That night, I had a nightmare. I dreamt that I lost my job at Phitzer for writing poetry on the job. I was walking in a daze on some street in Manhattan. I looked like I was purposeless, but I was actually looking for a job. I was leaving my resume on receptionists' desks, but nothing was happening. A wave of nausea overcame me as I realized I had been blacklisted by the industry. It was a small industry and word traveled fast. No one would give me an interview let alone a job, and I was hungry. I looked in my wallet and there was only one dollar in it. A dollar in

Manhattan won't get you very far. I awoke with sweat all over my face and realized that this was one possible future reality. I had to change or this was my future. Screw my artistic streak; I didn't want this reality.

Max and I went to breakfast and I told him about my dream. He said I was paranoid and that all I needed was to get laid. I told him he wasn't living in the real world yet.

I drove back to New Rochelle to face another day of reality in the Big Apple. I walked into my apartment, fed Sam, and thought about the millions of other people in Manhattan who were just getting by, living paycheck to paycheck. I thought about the high-living socialites who didn't give a damn about the rest of us. I started to hate New York. I didn't grow up here—why the hell should I stay here? I longed for the quieter environment and slower pace of Philadelphia. It was time to start polishing off the old resume.

CHAPTER

37

B ack at work, I had a breakthrough thought. No matter what happened to me, I should never feel sorry for myself. What about the road black Americans have had to travel? Or how about the tragedies of native Americans? My grief was but a speck of dust compared to their stories. As I walked down the halls at Phitzer, I didn't see any of these people. Everybody was white and middle-class or upper-middle-class. I started to feel ashamed of myself for having such a privileged life due to the color of my skin and the fact that I had parents who could send me to college. And if I was living so precariously, I couldn't imagine how people not of my race were making it.

I started thinking about how disenfranchised they must feel, seeing all this wealth all around them and having to struggle so hard to get just a small piece of it. I could see the source of their anger. Even though slavery had been eliminated well over a hundred years ago, blacks were still struggling with racial inequality. And native Americans had been relegated to the nation's hinterlands to keep them out of sight. Where was their piece of the American pie?

As I sat there at my desk thinking about these things, I started to not care so much about my job. I had no family, I had no wife. There was no reason for me to try to keep up with the Jones. My liberal upbringing had made me sympathetic to the underprivileged, and I wanted to walk in their shoes to <u>feel</u> how it felt to come from the wrong side of the tracks. I was now free to do whatever I wanted, and I wanted this. I started thinking about how I could lose my job, and I realized the best way was probably to do something else besides work on the job— perhaps poetry!

I sat at my desk and thought about how one from the underclass would feel about my job if he or she had it. I felt a poem coming on, and my mind went with the flow. Here it is:

Kill Whitey

There once was a Shawnee pharmacist
Who wrote NDAs for a living
His reputation preceded him from coast to coast
He was known for all his giving.

The money he made went back to his tribe

Who lived in Oklahoma
But it turned out that he had lied
On his resume; he was really a Shoshone.

He never went to Pharmacy school
He was a brazen practitioner
Of shamanistic medicine—oh what fools
They were to hire him—he was really a falconer.

For twenty years he plied his trade
No one of his bosses the wiser
That his resume was of lies made up
And his credentials came from an internal advisor.

When they found him out he left the trade
And went back to Oklahoma,
But all the mistakes he made
Left their mark, so once again he became a Sooner.

The FDA approved many of the drugs
That he said were safe and effective
But in reality they were dopes
For believing a twisted Shoshone bent on invective.

People were dying left and right
After the bad drugs made it to market
That Shoshone pharmacist had left a blight
And no one had ever called him on the carpet.
With satisfaction he headed back

West Knowing he had put up quite a fight
He knew he had done his best
To kill Whitey.

I stored this poem on my computer in a conspicuous place and wondered how long it would be before someone discovered it. I was laying landmines with which to eventually blow myself up. I had a job death wish, and I knew that eventually one of my landmines would succeed in its task. It was only a matter of time.

I didn't have to wait long for the shit to hit the fan. I had to take a personal day for Sam to get his shots. When I returned to work the next day I could feel a different vibe. A friendly co-worker warned me that Dr. Margolis had to retrieve a document from my computer while I was gone, and he discovered something he didn't like. The co-worker advised me to watch my back today.

I was prepared for battle. I knew what was coming and I steeled myself. Sure enough, fifteen minutes later Dr. Margolis called me into his office. I walked down the hall to his office and sat down in the chair closest to his desk. He handed me a sheet of paper. It was a copy of Kill Whitey.

"Did you write this at work?" he asked. "Yes, I did," I replied.

"You are supposed to be analyzing data at work, not writing poetry," Dr. Margolis said.

"I know, but sometimes I just can't help myself," I said.

"Well, you leave me no choice but to fire you," Dr. Margolis said. "This is a pharmaceutical company, not an advertising agency," he said. "Perhaps that is where you belong," he added.

"Yes, sir," I said. "I'm sorry I let you down, Dr. Margolis," I replied.

"I'm afraid I can't give you a good recommendation either," Dr. Margolis said. "You should have known better than this. Please give me your badge."

I did know better than this. I had planted my own bomb and today it went off. I walked out of his office and down the hall to the elevator. Fortunately, the elevator was already there. When I got to the lobby, I walked straight to the revolving door and never looked back.

It was with a mixture of sorrow, fear, and relief that I walked out onto the street. I had planted the seeds of my own destruction, and today those seeds came to fruition. I was now free, but I was also poor. I cherished my freedom but not my poverty. Unemployment would last six months, after which I would be a true pauper. At least I had six months before I had to live the true down-and-out lifestyle.

CHAPTER

The people at the unemployment office were a true cross-section of the down and out. Most had working-class clothes on and the majority were either black or Hispanic. I stuck out like a sore thumb. After filling out all my paperwork I was told it would be a couple of weeks before they would have their decision. I drove back to my apartment in New Rochelle and wondered what I was going to do with myself while I awaited unemployment's decision. There was always poetry.

Now I was free of the constraints of a job, and I knew I was about to face economic constraints that I had never experienced before. Unemployment, if I got it, would be half of my regular salary. If I was careful, I could keep my apartment and still feed Sam and myself. If I wasn't, I'd have to find a cheaper apartment and give Sam back to the shelter. I decided to be careful.

One day, I took the train to the Bronx Zoo. I was impressed by the size of their pens (now called "habitats"). They were well fed and well groomed and they performed no work. I thought of all the people who worked in much smaller cages every day. That was their life. They worked in their cages eight, ten, twelve hours a day, and then they came home and did their household chores. I was very recently one of them. This lifestyle didn't allow time for literature, philosophy, or any of the nobler arts. I was glad to be done with it.

Half of the jobs performed by humans could be performed by robots—why not use them?

I had seen enough, and I felt a poem coming on, so I hopped a train back to New Rochelle. The poem wouldn't wait until I got back home, so I had to write it on the train. It was only a little ditty, and here it is:

Autopilot

Who are we? Human beings.

Were we built to perform drudgery from dawn to dusk?

Were we meant to sit in an office eight, ten, twelve hours a day and push pencils?

I think not.

We're smart enough now to build robots

To do these things for us.

Man against machine, a conflict as old as H.G. Wells. I got home and hugged Sam and swore to him that I would never let myself become a machine again.

They decided favorably on my unemployment, so I had six months to learn how to be very poor. That is, poor financially, but rich in freedom.

I started off my days walking Sam. After that, I would drive to the New Rochelle Diner and compose poetry for several hours. I learned how to make a cup of coffee last two hours to keep my bill down. I discovered that I was a morning writer. The poetry that I wrote at the diner in the mornings was much better than the poetry I had written after work.

The new task at hand was to find a new balance in my unemployed days. I didn't want to spend my whole day writing in the diner; on the other hand, I couldn't afford to spend all day every day in Manhattan. The compromise I came up with was to spend half my day at the diner and half at the Free Library of New York where I wouldn't spend any money. All this required was transportation costs.

For the first two weeks of my unemployment, I was happy with this arrangement. I was living very cheaply and I was still experiencing the sights and sounds of New York. At night, when there was a poetry event, I would go and commiserate with other poets how difficult life had become.

I started to realize that my poetry was right in tune with the "mix." I was experiencing the same difficulties of life as other poets, and because we were poets we saw these difficulties more clearly. Babies born with AIDS, crack cocaine addiction, the divorce rate, and unfulfilled dreams were common themes, and with our poetry, we always shed new light on these subjects.

Slowly but surely, poets were no longer being scoffed at but were listened to and appreciated. I was slowly gaining a reputation in the poetry community. I knew this was my true calling and I had to follow it even if it meant a life of poverty. And for some reason, I wasn't afraid of this possibility. I hadn't been raised rich, and I knew how to stretch a dollar.

My pharmaceutical career was over, and I would have to find a new way to help support myself. New York was the publishing capital of the world, but I didn't want to be some assistant editor in a publishing house. I'd rather be a freelance writer. I decided to start writing articles and send them in to different magazines. I could work at my own pace and make as much as I wanted to. At last, I had a new plan.

CHAPTER

Sometimes I would sit in the New York Public Library figuring out how to get through the rest of the day on five dollars. The cycle of poverty and writing was difficult to figure out. George Orwell didn't figure it out in his lifetime. Most didn't. Only the fabulously lucky did.

I couldn't figure it out. All I knew was that my artistic streak had caused me to feel the sting of poverty. My desire to experience the underbelly of modern American life had left me divorced, alone, and unloved. There was no turning back on this path. The only future I had left was to fully explore this empty path and hope that there was a rainbow at the end of it. There was no rainbow yet in sight, but I was just starting out on this path.

In the meantime, as I walked past the street beggars, I realized that I was only one unemployment check ahead of them. In six months, I could very well be one of them. A college education was no longer a guarantee of success in life. There were now Ph.D.s working at Mcdonald's.

Only those born to wealth were immune from poverty in the new economy.

My only hope now was to write a brilliant novel or a brilliant screenplay. I knew that no one ever became rich writing poetry, but I continued to do it anyway because I enjoyed it. I had outgrown the nine-to-five routine, and there was no other way for me to become wealthy other than to write the great American novel or win the lottery. I wasn't a ruthless person; the only thing I had going for me was talent. I just didn't have that New York killer shark mentality; I knew I would have to succeed in life by different means. One good thing about New York is that it toughens your skin. If I did succeed as a writer, I would know how to handle the barbs of critics and nasty rejection letters from acquisitions editors.

Since getting fired, I knew that my writing had gotten better. Unfettered by the burdens of a nine-to-five job, my mind had the freedom to pursue those flights of fancy and bring them back down to Earth on a piece of paper. With time now on my side, my imagination could linger longer on my conceits, and I had the time to express them as clearly as possible. I felt like a fledgling just learning how to fly. The only obstacle I had to overcome was poverty.

I was now living the literary life, and I loved it, except for the poverty part. Poverty did not become me, and I knew that I had to start making money writing or my dream of being a successful author would fade. When I considered how much I had given up for this dream, I felt a sense of urgency to succeed. I wanted to prove to the world that an artistic streak was still worth having. If no one had one, there would be no literature, no art, no music, no joy in life. I didn't want to live in a world without these things. Even more, I wanted to contribute to the arts. I wanted to be somebody who had something to say.

Nowhere in the country was there a more active arts scene than in New York. And yet, there was something perverse about it. How many were young scions of industry moguls with nothing better to do with their time? There was so much money in New York, and it was difficult to tell the struggling artist from the pampered socialite. I hated rich New Yorkers. They were so faux. There were also so many rich sons and daughters of famous people riding the gravy train of their family name. Of course, there were also the Madonnas, who made it on their own. These were the ones I admired.

Since I was not from a wealthy family, I knew that the only way I was going to make it was on my own. And this being New York, I was up against the big guns— Norman Mailer, E.L. Doctorow, and Kurt Vonnegut, Jr. I doubted very much if I would ever achieve their kind of literary fame, but I could always dream.

The most important thing I had to work on right now was my discipline. I forced myself to put two hours in every morning at the diner and another three hours in at the public library. Even if I felt writer's block coming on, I would stay until my time was up. Thus, I lived a very regimented life even though I was unemployed. They say that one can only find freedom through discipline, and now I knew what that meant. The difference was that now I was spending every second of the day the way I wanted to. I was finally living life on my terms, instead of on some company's terms, and I liked the feeling that gave me.

Three months into my unemployment, I had a novel half completed. I was pretty proud of it, and I couldn't wait to finish it so that I could send it to a literary agent.

Even though I was unemployed, I spent my days at work hoping for the big pay-off.

CHAPTER

When I got tired of working on my novel, I switched to poetry to get the motor going again. For three months, I had written very little poetry because I had been making such good progress on my novel. Finally, one day I hit a doldrums, and I put on my poetic hat. I still couldn't come up with anything, so I started writing a short story. It was about my experiences on the speaker's committee when I was in college. It was about how I learned not to be afraid of speaking in public to a lot of people. I thought it was a pretty good story, so when I got home I put it in the bottom drawer of my desk. I thought that it might be part of a short story anthology someday.

I decided to go on a short story kick. I was so happy with my first result that I wanted to add to my anthology immediately. My second venture in this genre was a story

I had heard through the grapevine about something that happened to somebody who worked for a big eight accounting firm. I wrote it in the first person as though it was my story.

I thought that this story was good enough for my future anthology so I put it in my desk drawer with the other story. Someday, I knew that I would have a publishable short story anthology.

After this interlude of short stories, I went back to my main endeavor—my novel. My goal was to finish my novel before my unemployment ran out because then I would probably have to go back to work.

Sometimes I wish I had never developed an artistic streak. If I had no artistic streak, perhaps I would still be married to Lauren and not be thinking about George Orwell all the time. I do not believe that intellectuals are born; they become intellectuals with effort. They learn and think and ponder and eventually learn to appreciate the beauty of the human mind. This requires skill and dedication. I was proud to be an intellectual. Screw the world—I am a thinker.

It is with this attitude that I approached my novel anew. I wanted that hard, biting edge in my book. I wanted to poke a hole in reality as we know it and get people to stop throwing their lives away on the job. I wanted people to STOP!, look, and listen.

For the next few days, I had that hard edge, and I put it into my book. I kept pushing on, relishing the completion of each sentence. I pushed on day after day for a straight month, until I was almost finished with my novel. And then for some reason, I can't explain, with only a chapter to go, I felt the urge to take a hiatus and write some poetry. I had heard through the poetry community that Yorick had to be hospitalized in a mental institution. He had gone off his medication and became psychotic. I put myself in his shoes and wrote this poem about him:

Damaged Goods

And so I sit alone in my hospital room
And wonder why my serotonin and dopamine receptors
Got so out of whack that I wound up here
With other whackos whose neurotransmitters got out of whack.

They put me on Risperdal then switched it to Seroquel
To quell the paranoid thoughts and hallucinations
I thought to myself—this is pretty close to Hell
To have nothing to do but think about how crazy you are.

It wasn't always like this I thought to myself
I knew halcyon days when everything was beautiful
I had a beautiful wife and a beautiful home
Nestled in the rolling hills overlooking the valley.

How lucky was I, a half-breed from New Mexico
To snag a Main Line charm school girl
And travel the world on company money
Then come home to a wife and family.

But slowly my neurotransmitters got out of whack
And I started hearing things
Things like: you're doing a lousy job,
You don't belong here, you're a fake.

When I lost my job, it was the final straw
My wife couldn't take it anymore
So she left, and found another man
Who didn't have trouble with his neurotransmitters.

The pain and loneliness only made matters worse
The drugs just couldn't get the right balance
Old memories of Viet Nam haunted me
My wife pretty much wanted me dead.

So alone now I face the world
Risperdal and Seroquel percolating in my brain
Looking for the right balance to keep me sane
And somehow I've aged twenty years in two.

Maybe I married over my head
Maybe I should have married within my own tribe
But on the East Coast, where would I find my Pocahontas?

Where would I find my Sacagawea? I'm in the wrong
neighborhood.
I used to be a fine young man when my chemicals were intact
I made my parents very proud that coming from a little shack
I conquered upper society and lived a charmed life
If only for a little while, before my mental illness attack.

If only mental illness didn't run in my family
I might have ruled the world
Instead I sit here on this hospital bed
And shiver, because my new world is so cold.

After reading the poem over and over, I realized why I
had to write it. There was only a fine line of difference
between Yorick and me. Like Yorick, lived alone and
explored the outer reaches of human consciousness, but
unlike Yorick, I did not have a chemical imbalance. I was
not psychotic without medication. I thanked my lucky
stars for that every day after I heard about Yorick.

CHAPTER

With three weeks of my unemployment left, I finished my novel. Now the fun part started— finding a publisher or at least a literary agent. Through my poetry connections, I had met a literary agent—Lynne Carroll—who told me to send her my novel when I was finished with it. I did this and hoped for the best.

In the meantime, I polished off my resume because I knew if I didn't get a job within a month I would starve. Fortunately for me, one of the few docs at Phitzer who liked me had moved on to a company located in Princeton, New Jersey. I decided to send his company a copy of my resume on the off chance that they needed someone with my expertise.

Politely, I also nudged Lynne Carroll for feedback— good or bad. I was very anxious to see if she thought there was a market for my writing. I marked each day that went by off the calendar, with there being more tension each day that I didn't hear from her.

I called Dr. Feingold at the company in Princeton and told him that I was interested in the open position. So much for freedom. Economic security had won out over the desire to be an artist. I still didn't know if I was a promising artist or not, and I felt like I needed to get back on a schedule anyway. I realized that I didn't have the courage of George Orwell after all. My courage was a sham. I was a sell-out. If I got the job in Princeton, I would take it and work like hell just like everybody else. I wanted a steady income again and I wanted to confirm. My artistic streak had led me down a different path, but now I wanted to get back on the straight and narrow.

Somebody from Human Resources from the company in Princeton called me to tell me that I had gotten an interview. That made my day.

The day after my interview in Princeton, Lynne called. She liked the book! Thank God, she liked the book! She said she needed time to think about which publishing company to pitch it to. She said she wasn't sure if she wanted to go straight to the big guns or take a subtler approach. But she liked it!

That whole day I walked around on cloud nine, I treated Sam to a feast, and I called Max to tell him the news. Suddenly, I felt invincible. I had beaten the odds or was about to. The Force was with me, and I even had a good feeling about that job in Princeton. After a bad run for the last couple of years, things were turning around. I had thought that I would be down and out for the rest of my life, but maybe that wasn't my fate. Maybe God had better plans for me.

The next day I had even better news. Dr. Feingold's clout at the company in Princeton had been strong enough to get me the job. I could start the day after my unemployment ran out.

CHAPTER

All I needed now was a new place to live somewhere around Princeton. Of course, Princeton was very expensive too. I'd have to find a cheap apartment somewhere outside town.

Things were suddenly looking up for me. From Princeton, my friends were within easy commuting distance. In addition, I liked the whole art scene in the New Hope/Lambertville area.

Princeton—it had a nice ring to it. I had visions of ivy-covered halls, students carrying sacks of books, and long philosophical discourses on grass-covered lawns. It sounded perfect for me.

I couldn't find an apartment in Princeton for less than a thousand a month, which was over a third of my take-home pay. Still, I was excited to be returning closer to home turf. New York had done nothing but brutalize me, and at least I would be closer to my friends in Philadelphia. Philadelphia is where I had met the love of my life and New York is where I lost her. From Princeton, halfway between the two cities, my heart would always look south.

I had experienced the triumph of riches in Philadelphia and the curse of poverty in New York. There is no more pitiful a sight than a down-and-out New Yorker. From Princeton, I could wipe the slate clean, start afresh, and look forward to the joys of living again.

I thought of all the famous people who had lived in Princeton—number one being Albert Einstein of course. I promised myself that I would take the time to visit the Advanced Institute of Physics where he taught. Princeton was also home to the brilliant mathematician John Nash. At one point in time, the other brilliant physicist Richard Feynman taught at Princeton. I'm sure there were many more, but I couldn't think of them.

All I knew was that I was excited as hell to be moving to Princeton. Even though I had been blackballed in the industry in New York, I guess that curse didn't travel that far south to Princeton. Even "dropping out" to write a novel couldn't dissuade Dr. Feingold from thinking highly of me. I guess I wasn't such an asshole after all.

CHAPTER

One week before I was to start my new job I got a call from Lynne. Random House wanted to publish my book! She was in the process of negotiating a contract, but they loved it and definitely wanted to go ahead. I thanked Lynne and told her that I wanted to treat her to dinner. She reversed the tables on me and insisted that she treat me to dinner. I didn't object; after all, she would make money on the deal too. She asked if Friday night was good for me. I said that it was.

The intervening days were a blur of positive energy and planning. I was so happy to be leaving New Rochelle. I never felt at home here. I was sick and tired of living in Westchester County. At least people in Princeton made it because of their brain power, not their family's fortune.

I put on my blue wool sports coat and khaki pants for my "date" with Lynne. I took the train to Penn Station and started walking towards Morton's Steakhouse. I was looking forward to a juicy steak and Caesar salad.

I entered the restaurant and looked around for Lynne. I saw her sitting alone at a table near the back of the restaurant. She was wearing a blue suit with a red scarf. She looked very patriotic.

"You know," she said with a smile, "I can probably get you an advance on your next book."

"I'm not sure there's going to be a next book," I said. "I had to go back to work. I was having a hard time feeding my dog."

"Surely you're exaggerating," Lynne said.

"No, really, there were days when I didn't know where my next meal was coming from," I replied.

"Well, all that's over now," she said. "I wouldn't be surprised if your book made you a millionaire. And you can't stop writing now—soon you'll be a household name and people will want more from you," she added.

"Well, until I have a million in the bank, I'll be working in Princeton," I said.

"What about me?" she asked. "I had to knock down some heavy doors for Random House to take a chance on you. That took a lot of work. Don't tell me you're going to stop laying the golden eggs now," she said in a harsh tone.

"I have started an anthology of short stories I'd like to finish," I said.

"Fine," Lynne said. "Once your name is out there I can market just about anything you give me," she said.

"I'll get to work on it right away and I'll give you a call when it's done," I said.

She seemed satisfied with that and she quieted down and went back to eating her steak. I went back to my steak too thinking about the anthology. I knew that an anthology of short stories wasn't as marketable as a novel, but I just didn't have another novel in me right now. Better to go back and regroup with short fiction I thought to myself.

I looked up at Lynne. Her blond hair just touched her red scarf. She had more make-up on than usual and I wondered if she was trying to look pretty for me. She had never given me even a hint that she might be interested in me. Our relationship had been consummately professional, and I assumed that was the way she liked it. But what if I was wrong? What if she secretly had the hots for me now that I was a soon-to-be-published author? Was I missing a great opportunity to extend our relationship?

With these thoughts in mind, I finished my dinner first and looked up at Lynne. I got nothing from her body language. Why do women have to be so God damn mysterious? She finished her meal and asked our waiter for the check.

"Did you enjoy the meal?" she asked. "Very much, thank you," I replied.

"I'll pitch the anthology idea to Random House and see what they think," she said.

"I'll keep you updated how it's coming," I said. "Good," she replied.

She paid the bill, leaving the waiter a nice tip. I stood up and walked around the table to pull her chair out. She appreciated the gesture and said thank you.

We walked through the restaurant and stepped through the door and out onto the street. I realized that she didn't know what to say to bring the evening to a close. After an awkward silence, I said, "Thank you Lynne for a wonderful evening." And I meant it.

CHAPTER

I started my job in Princeton with the confidence of knowing that my new book would be coming out within a couple of months. Having suffered the pangs of poverty for six months, I felt such a debt of gratitude to Dr. Feingold that I practically fawned over him. He knew that I was hamming it up, but he appreciated it nonetheless.

Knowing that I was going to be earning money again, I rented an old farmhouse just outside of Princeton. It was much nicer than my apartment in New Rochelle, and Sam loved it. The farmhouse sat on ten acres of land and I let Sam have the run of it.

I was friendly with everybody in the company, and soon everybody liked me. Nothing was held against me that had happened at Phitzer. I was truly given a fresh chance to start over again. I would work on my short story anthology at my own pace and I wouldn't let my artistic streak get the better of me. I was now in firm control of it, and I knew that's the way it had to be for the rest of my life.

I was "in the zone" at work, but when I came home I didn't think about work at all. I truly enjoyed the area where I lived, especially Lambertville and Frenchtown. The stretch of road between these two towns was a cyclist's paradise. The road had ten-foot shoulders on both sides, and there were some beautiful vistas of the Delaware River. I bought a bicycle and rode the stretch every chance I got.

When I felt creative, I started a short story. Within a month of starting my new job, I had started at least five short stories.

Even though I was living alone, my life was in balance and harmony. During the best hours of the day, I put my mind into my work and did the best I could. When I came home in the evening I allowed my right brain the freedom it wanted. I let myself follow its whimsy and do things I normally wouldn't do. Left brain at work and right brain at home and somehow it worked, or at least it worked for me.

I had also gotten together with Max. Max was dating a new girlfriend as usual, and the three of us got together for dinner. Her name was Kathy Cola and she was a bubbly, effervescent blond. She looked a little like Lynne, except that Lynne was serious and not effervescent.

We all had a great meal, and Max told Kathy that I had a new book coming soon. It turned out that Kathy was the manager of a bookstore, and she would have me in for a signing. I was very excited about this stroke of luck, and even Max thought I was lucky.

I really liked Kathy. There was nothing phony about her, and I thought that Max was very lucky. She genuinely wanted me to succeed as a writer, and I really appreciated that. I liked the perky, bubbly personality, and the fact that she enjoyed helping people.

Max saw this quality in her and I think that's the reason he fell for her. I would have fallen for her too but he found her first. The truth of the matter is that I wasn't even looking. Until I was one hundred percent sure that I had my artistic streak fully under control, I didn't even want to look at a woman.

I was finally starting to learn who I really was. I realized that I had a wonderful mind. Albert Einstein once wrote that imagination is more important than knowledge, and I was a living, breathing testimony to this idea. Within my mind was a vast wonderland of the imagination, and all I had to do was control it so that I could live successfully in the real world. And I was getting better at this. I was living at the spot on this planet where that statement originated from, and I was living its truth.

I started to realize that I had lost Lauren not because of my imaginative capacity, but because of my inability to control it. I had not matured enough for that.

I was living in a place where SCIENCE was king, and I actually fit in quite well into this paradigm. However, beyond this immediate reality was the unending panorama of limitless imagination. The key to success, for me, was to keep these two worlds in harmony.

CHAPTER

I started reading Down and Out in Paris and London again. This time I was looking at it strictly as an economic analysis of a young artist's life. After all, that was its theme. And then I expanded on this theme and realized that one facet of every person's life was an economic analysis. What made George Orwell so different was that he was an incredible artist who could tell his story so well.

I had never experienced the depravity of poverty until I spent six unemployed months in New York. Ironically, those six months could insulate me from poverty for the rest of my life if my book does well.

Of course, it was doubtful that my book would make me a millionaire. With any luck, maybe it would make me a thousandaire. Still, that was better than being a pauper.

Of course, there were many other writers and thinkers besides George Orwell who presented their ideas on economic analysis of lives. The first of these was Adam Smith, whose The Wealth of Nations in 1776 really started the social science of economics. Other nonfiction greats on the subject were Karl Marx and John Maynard Keynes. Karl Marx's ideas eventually spawned the communist revolution, while Keynes' work definitely established economics as a science.

In the world of fiction, great writers like Jane Austin, Charles Dickens, and John Steinbeck portrayed the class struggles and impoverishment of characters caught in the web of poverty. But what I like about George Orwell is that as far as I know, he is the first writer to write a nonfiction work in the form of a personal narrative and elevate it to the status of a work of art. He is the face of poverty, telling his own true story of his early struggles with poverty.

I realized that during my six months of unemployment in New York I never came close to the abject poverty that George Orwell endured and that the main reason for this was my education. I was a college graduate. I could live down and out for a while and then polish the old resume and get a job, which is exactly what I did.

There was a parallel between George Orwell and myself. Because of his education, even at the times when he felt the most degradation, people considered him a "gentleman." Because of this distinction, he was treated with special favor. His class distinction as gentleman meant that he was a man just temporarily down on his luck and that things could improve for him at any moment. I realized that the same distinction applies today. Being a college graduate meant that I did not have to be a permanent member of the underclass. My college degree was my ticket to upward mobility, and even if I temporarily found myself down and out, I could use my ticket to get out of a jam.

At least this was true at the time I am writing this. I do not know if this will remain true forever. As I said previously, there are Ph.D.s holding down jobs at Mcdonald's now, so the future of education is not all bright and rosy. But at least it holds true up to the end of the twentieth century.

CHAPTER

I finished reading Down and Out in Paris and London again and I know that my observations about education and class were true. The big difference between George and me was that he went through his trials with poverty absolutely alone. I did too, but constantly in the back of my mind were my experiences with Lauren and the constant what-ifs. What if I had made more money—would she have stayed? What if I had tried to please her more— would she have stayed with me? That's where our take on our experiences differed. And recognizing this difference led me to explore the relationship between women and economics further.

My first conclusion was that there was a fundamental difference between what women want and what men want. First of all, women are nesting birds and need to build nests. Men, on the other hand, are non-nesting birds and like to be "free as a bird." Thus, the fundamental difference between men and women. Women want "men of substance" who can provide a nice nest, while men want supermodels or nymphomaniacs. Women are attracted to doctors and CEOs because they are men of substance who make a lot of money and can provide nice nests. Men, for the most part, just want the cutest girl in the neighborhood in order to satisfy their sexual appetite. Of course, not all men have brains and there are other types of men that women want. Some high-powered women want men who are good with their hands—men who know how to fix things. They are easily controlled and rarely talk back. That's why some women want men in prison—they are perfectly controlled in their environment and are grateful at the least prospect of interest.

Only dumb women want handsome men. Men by nature have a roving eye, and the handsomer they are, the more likely they are to attract women and find sexual success. Women tend to not like thinkers, which is why so many intellectual men are divorced. Women want doers, not thinkers. If a man can fix the car or the kitchen sink, he is valuable in a woman's eye. Writers, in particular, usually have a terrible time with women. Writers tend to live in an abstract world that most women just don't get.

Then there are "weak" men. Only a small minority of women like weak men. Weak men usually fall into one of two categories. The first type is the kind who is looking for a mother figure. Maybe they didn't get enough love from Mommy growing up or maybe they just have an Oedipal complex. The other type of weak man is the type who is looking for a "ticket" into a certain socioeconomic class. If he is from the lower-middle class, he wants a wife from the upper-middle class to bolster his socioeconomic standing.

Both types are weak men, and most women dismiss them early on.

What it all boils down to is that men's and women's genes are fundamentally different. In some ways, it is a miracle that we have been able to perpetuate the species at all. If it weren't for sex drive, none of us would probably be here.

It is the children of the future that I worry about. The current divorce rate is already close to sixty percent. Most children today are the product of divorced parents. The trend does not seem to be getting any better, and many people are wondering if the whole institution of marriage is obsolete. The trendsetters seem to think so.

The fifty and sixty-year marriages of the World War II generation are slowly becoming extinct. In this day of instant gratification, people treat lovers like used cars. When they have a certain amount of mileage on them they are traded in for something newer. In my own personal experience, I guess I should be grateful. Who wants to be married to someone who wants to trade them in?

Such were my rambling thoughts on modern-day relationships. I couldn't help but see my marriage in a different light. I realized that perhaps my ex-wife classified me as a weak man, either because of my artistic streak or maybe because she thought I was using her as a "ticket" to that stratum of society. Whatever the case, I lost her, and whether I understood why or not didn't matter anymore.

CHAPTER

Sometimes I missed the hubbub of New York City, but mostly not. Actually, I liked Princeton so much better. It had the same intellectual timbre of New York City without the emotional stress. It really was the perfect climate for me.

I wish I had done better financially in New York. I could have moved into a better apartment in Princeton and had more room. But I didn't, and it was like I was starting from scratch. Starting from scratch. Brand new beginning. I knew that I had to remain in that mindset in order to conquer my past. My life had to become a tabula rasa again in order for me to succeed in the future. Writers know that writing is therapeutic, and they are right. I felt like a new man with the weight of the world off my shoulders since finishing my book. It was spring, and everything was blossoming anew. I wanted to make my life an eternal spring, full of endless wonderful possibilities.

Dr. Feingold was very happy with my work. He saw the effort I put into being focused every day, and he spoke highly of me to top management. As a consequence, I was given a nice bonus. That bonus was good for three months' rent.

Lynne Carroll sent me the pre-release promotional material for my book. It was very clever and the graphic artwork was quite good. I looked forward with anticipation to its release date, and so did Lynne.

I didn't expect to make a lot of money on the book, but enough to make my life a little more comfortable. More importantly, it was my entrée into the world of big-time publishing. Having had a book published by Random House put me one up on other aspiring young writers. Lynne knew this, which is why she kept encouraging me to write. She had a monetary stake in my future too.

As I discovered during my six unemployed months in New York, the writer's life isn't such a great life when you don't know where your next meal is coming from. Thank heaven for Baxter Laboratories and Dr. Feingold. I was put in charge of all clinical pharmacology documentation and I was good at it. I became known as the go-to man pertaining to anything to do with clinical pharmacology documentation. Not only did this give me a role in the real world, it was also very financially rewarding. I was making about seventy-five thousand a year and could afford just about anything I wanted.

I joined a gym. Even though I ran four miles every night after work on the horse track behind the farmhouse, I felt that I also needed weight training. I was in top cardiovascular health, and I also wanted to make my thirty-five-year-old body as perfect a specimen as it could possibly be.

Lynne called to say that my book came out today. She told me she would like to see my next book within the next two months. I told her that my job took a lot of my energy but that I would try.

I went through my days thinking about making my body and mind as strong as they would possibly be. I do not know why my mindset took this course, but it felt right. I started to realize that I was becoming whole again, even though I was by myself. I was learning again how to be a complete self by myself. I had to make myself strong again. I needed to have a complete yin and a complete yang within myself.

CHAPTER

The same slogan that applies to real estate also applies to real life—location, location, location. I had been down and out in Philadelphia and New York, but now I was on top of my game in Princeton. I liked feeling like part of a team again, working towards the common good. I was being appreciated for my hard work and I was being financially very well rewarded. Being part of a team again made me see how lonely a writer's life can be. Working in solitude is one of the most difficult ways to spend one's life imaginable. But thank God for those artists and visionaries who are willing to sacrifice so much to tell us the truth about the human condition. Where would we be without them?

I had stuck my neck out for six months to be like them, and I found it a very difficult place to be. I had felt the pangs of hunger and poverty for the first time in my life, and I really feel like it is something everyone should have the courage to do at some point in their life. To step out of the socioeconomic whirlpool and experience life in the raw takes courage. I had found that courage for a hundred and eighty days, and during that time I had produced a work of art—a book. Had I not taken a step back, I never would have been able to do it.

The writer's life is filled with ups and downs, just like everybody else's. What keeps the writer going is his intellect and love of the brilliant minds that have gone before him. The love lives of writers are usually difficult because they tend to be unconventional. Most writers suffer from a form of solipsism. Some are willing to die for their art. The art of fine writing requires so much concentration and effort that they have to withdraw into themselves to produce their best, often to the detriment of those around them. If it's so difficult and causes so much pain, why do it? Because sometimes the end result is a work of magnificent beauty, and that is the reason why we were put on this earth, to magnify God's beauty. And unfortunately, to do this really well usually requires a good amount of suffering. It's unfortunate, but necessary to the process.

I do not know what the limits of other writers have been, but I knew my own limit to be six months. Perhaps I am a coward. Better writers than myself have suffered their entire lives for their art, some never attaining any recognition. I had hopes that my first book would at the least put me on the literary map. At least I would know if this was going to happen or not within the next several months.

In the meantime, I had a good job, Dr. Feingold still liked me, and I was starting to get my masculine confidence back again. I had several dates with a girl named Lynn, and I had slept with her. The sex was good and she was quite accommodating, but my heart wasn't in it and she knew it. The next time we got together she dumped me. I didn't really care, because she was right, I wasn't ready for a serious relationship. At least I got laid.

Lynne Carroll called to tell me that there was a review of my book in Publishers Weekly. Overall, the review was positive. Lynne assured me that Random House was doing everything in its power to market the book. That made me very happy because although I had an MBA in marketing, I knew I was hopeless at marketing.

I filled my days doing the best job I could at work and my nights reading book reviews. In the farmhouse I rented, I had a grand piano in the living room, along with a giant wide-screen TV, and I had a hot tub in the greenhouse that connected to the living room. I would sit in the hot tub for hours at a time reading.

Only a mile or two up Route 31 was a strip club named Easy Street. Sometimes after work, I would sip beer and watch sleazy women gyrate in front of me, and then I would go home and masturbate into a condom in the hot tub. Thank God I didn't have children.

CHAPTER

D ating in Princeton after living in New York is like fishing in a twelve by twelve-foot pond as opposed to the ocean. Especially for people in their thirties. Everyone already has a life or is getting a life or has given up on getting a life. Everyone, that is, except me. I was in a state of limbo. I was dating and trying to get a new life, but I was doing so half-heartedly. I wanted a new woman, but nobody lived up to Lauren.

In essence, all I had was hope, and that was what I lived on, and that hope allowed me to start thinking outside the box. I started thinking about all the women I knew, and who among them might make a suitable mate. And who among them slowly rose to the top of the list?—Lynne Carroll. She was single, she loved literature, and she was blond—the opposite of Lauren. She was tough, but she was also sexy. I could envision her keeping me sexually satisfied for the rest of my life.

Out of all the candidates, Lynne made the most sense. I decided to ask her out for Friday night. I told her to meet me at the Tavern on the Green in Central Park at seven p.m.

She was dressed in a low-cut aquamarine dress that accented her blond hair quite nicely. After ordering our aperitifs, she asked me how my next book was coming.

"Pretty slowly," I replied.

"Don't tell me you're going to be another one-shot wonder," she said.

"I hope not, but my new job does take up almost all of my energy," I replied.

"I've been given a mandate by the management of my company not to waste my time on authors who aren't prolific enough," she said. She added, "I hope you're not going to fall in that category."

I started in on my mussels marinara and said, "I don't think so. I just think it's going to take me longer now that I'm working."

She seemed to accept that and didn't say anything. She started in on her appetizer and looked around the room. Tavern on the Green was a place where the elite of New York come to eat. Riffraff did not come here because they couldn't afford it. I realized that because of my association with Lynne, I could appear to be one of New York's elite. This could change at any moment, of course, but for now it was true.

Lynne's words drifted over my head as I pursued this line of thought. I thought about how I had come down in the world. Losing a Main Line society girl is like losing all the air in your balloon. Instead of a beautiful work of art, all you have left is stretched rubber.

Despite these ruminations, I did not allow within myself room for self-pity. I felt lucky that I had such a ride because most people never experience what I experienced during their lifetime. The divorce had left me broken-hearted but not broken-spirited, and after all, was said and done, I was still a learned man. My brain was a resource that would allow me to try harder next time.

I was still in my mid-thirties, handsome, confident, and still full of adventure. I had many mountains yet to climb. I was not yet broken down with age. I had not suffered from malnutrition, and I was physically strong. But most importantly, I was free. My life was a tabla rosa again. I could go anywhere I wanted and do anything I wanted. He who travels alone travels farthest.

I looked at Lynne's eyes and slowly started coming back to planet earth. Her blue eyes sparkled in the candlelight and I felt very attracted to her. I let that thought go almost as soon as it came to me. Lynne was my agent, and I knew that she didn't want to be my girlfriend. It would probably ruin our business relationship if we became personally involved. So much that idea, I thought to myself.

Lynne finished eating and asked the waiter for the check. She said the meal was her treat and then she gave me a deadline—two months to finish my next book. I thought that was feasible and agreed to it. I thanked her for the meal and walked around the table to pull her chair out. She appreciated the gesture and offered her hand. I clasped it and shook it limply. Was it wrong on my part to want so much more?

CHAPTER

Towards the end of Down and Out in Paris and London George Orwell waxes philosophical about his views on money. In one very pertinent sentence, he writes, "Money has become the grand test of virtue." After reading that line, it struck me how true that thought was, and that perhaps it was even more true today than during Orwell's lifetime. It seems that everything today has become just another commodity. Things like faith, hope, and charity can now be bought and sold. Every celebrity in the country must have his or her favorite charity or the spin-doctors of the media will destroy them. Those with the money to become philanthropists are now the most virtuous people in the world.

Also during his philosophical discourse, he reflects on what he considers to be the three most powerful evils of poverty: hunger, an asexual existence, and idleness. Of hunger, he writes that it robs a man not only physically but also spiritually. I can easily see how this is true. If a man has hunger in his belly and he doesn't have the resources to pay for his next meal, he can think of nothing else. All appreciation of art or nature vanishes, and eventually so does rational thought. If this condition is a constant state, it becomes all-encompassing. The man can see no higher purpose, only survival. He lives on the animal level, and he no longer seeks beauty or truth.

As for an asexual existence, what woman from a decent upbringing wants to lower herself to live in poverty? It is not within a woman's evolutionary make-up to do so. She may flirt with it when she is young or naïve, but women cannot live outside of their nature forever. In the end, women will only stay with a prince.

Men in real poverty lose their sex drive anyway. They are so worried about their next meal they can't even begin to think about courting a woman. Proper courting of a woman not only takes time but also adequate resources. In today's highly competitive world, the minimum is that a man must have a job. However, each day the bar gets a little higher. There is now a big difference between a middle-class "professional" and a working-class man. Many more doors are open to the professional man than the uneducated working-class man. And in all honesty, it's even become more difficult for a professional man than ever because as women's minimum requirements become higher and higher, fewer men qualify. Writers like me and philosophers are being bred out of society—there simply isn't enough money in it, unless one is fabulously lucky.

Orwell's third and final trait of poverty—idleness—is a much more subtle topic than the previous two. It is hard to imagine anyone living in the modern world to be absolutely idle. Even beggars on the street must get up in the morning and go to work. I guess this pitfall of poverty is relative. Compared to an investment banker on Wall Street, a beggar does not work that hard. Here, a distinction must be made. Orwell was not talking about idleness per se, but forced idleness, like making the tramps wait for hours before they could enter the lodging house and forcing them to move from lodging house to lodging house each night. Perhaps the closest analogous situation to this today is unemployment. It is interesting that in today's society if one voluntarily leaves a job he or she is not entitled to compensation, but if one is fired from a job for gross incompetence or some other reason, he or she is entitled to unemployment compensation. Either way, that person is no longer viewed as a productive member of society, unless they are of retirement age, and then they are excused. Of course, millions of people are underemployed, but at least they are not idle. In today's society, it is better to be underemployed than unemployed. Writers are considered to be just one step above the unemployed, unless they are famous, in which case they are venerated.

What does all of this have to do with me? After thinking about Orwell's criteria for poverty, I realized that the only one I had suffered from was number two—an asexual existence, and even that was self-imposed for the most part. I had never really gone hungry and I was never idle. The only reason my success with women had been diminished was because I had been hurt. I was a wounded man, and women are not fools; they know a wounded man when they meet one. No amount of acting or chicanery can cover it up. The wound exists somewhere in ethereal space and the only thing that can heal a wound like that is a lot of time.

CHAPTER

I was blessed that I only had to experience one of the three evils of poverty that Orwell wrote about. And of the three, mine was definitely the least pernicious. As money started coming in from my book, I had a little more disposable income. On weekends, I started driving to Atlantic City, which was only an hour and a half away, and playing the blackjack tables. I usually broke even, but sometimes I would come out a couple of hundred dollars ahead or behind.

Gambling did nothing to diminish my smoking habit. If anything, it increased it. After I ran out of my own cigarettes, I would go scavenging around the casino for half-smoked or one-third-smoked cigarettes. It was a disgusting habit, and I always felt terrible while I was doing it, but I just couldn't bring myself to buy a new pack at twice the price I could get them at a convenience store. So like a bum, I would pick partially smoked cigarettes out of the ashtrays in the casino and store them in a little tin

Band-Aid box. The taste of an old cigarette was almost invariable terrible, but I did get the nicotine I craved into my system.

At home, I realized that I had the best of both worlds. I was living on a farm and had the beauty of nature all around me, while at the same time I had New York, Philadelphia, and Atlantic City all within roughly an hour's drive. These metropolises were far enough away that I could even see the stars at night quite clearly. It was difficult to see the Milky Way, but the stars and constellations were usually quite clear. One spring night, I walked to the other side of the pond in back of the farmhouse and saw my own zodiac sign—Scorpio—beaming quite clearly. I remembered from my childhood that the second star in Scorpio was Antares—right where the heart of the scorpion would be. I remembered that Antares was actually a binary star—the main star was a red giant, but there was also a much smaller blue dwarf revolving around it. In ancient Persia, Antares was the guardian star of the western sky. Now, it was simply the heart of Scorpio.

There was once a day on earth when men had the ability to see the colors of the stars with their bare eyes. A few remote tribes may still be able to do this, but for the most part, this ability is gone. On the other hand, we now have the Hubble space telescope orbiting the earth giving us images the likes of which men have never seen before. I have seen some of these images, and they are fantastic. They show that there is no limit to God's imagination.

If one has any doubt about God's imagination, just look at all the plants and animals He created. Maybe it's not limitless, but perhaps it could be. The thing about life forms is that they undergo evolution, where there is practically no limit on what life forms could be.

The scientific term for this phenomenon is biodiversity. This is a nice-sounding word for a very complex idea. It is still debatable whether or not biodiversity is increasing or decreasing with time. My own opinion is that it is decreasing. Just look at the dinosaurs. Only God really knows how many different species of dinosaurs there were. We know that all of them became extinct. How many other animals and plants have become extinct? My belief is that we will never know for sure.

The important thing was that now that I had pulled my first book up out of my gut, I had started thinking about the things that were really important—like biology. Where better than on a farm to start thinking about this subject?

CHAPTER

I started reading Biomedical Research News since I was working in that field. One of the interesting stories I came across was the story of Harry—one of the three Galapagos turtles that Charles Darwin brought back to England with him from the Galapagos Islands in 1826. Harry is still alive and lives in a zoo in Australia. In the 1920s, it was discovered that Harry was actually female, so they renamed him, Harriet. Harriet is still alive and is the oldest documented animal living on the planet.

I thought back to my days as a zoology student, and I remembered that I was a lousy zoologist. Too much memorization. However, I was a good botany student. For some reason, plants came alive for me while animals did not. The beautiful thing about botany is that through it it is possible to become self-supporting. In other words, you can grow your own. And it is possible to go even one step further. It is possible to achieve exaltation through farming. Not just any farming, but only through organic farming. This means using all-natural fertilizers and all-natural pesticides. In addition, it means that the fruits and vegetables must be hand-picked, not machine-picked. These are the minimum requirements. If one goes to the extreme, it also means using no mechanized machinery. The Amish of Lancaster County, Pennsylvania still use hand plows.

When I wasn't busy sucking up to Dr. Feingold during the day, at night I would walk out back to the pond and look up at the stars. I had read that there were only twenty-one first magnitude stars in the sky out of the infinite number of stars up there. I had memorized their names and their locations from a Sky and Telescope map. I could only find about half of them before I gave up. Still, that was more than most people knew.

I started thinking about the signs of the zodiac. Lauren was on the Virgo/Libra cusp and I was on the Scorpio/Sagittarius cusp. This means that we were on hexagonal points from each other on the zodiac map, which is good, but the most favorable astrological compatibility comes from trines. In my case, this means that I should be most compatible with either a Pisces or a Cancer.

Being in a hexagonal relationship is good but not the best. Our stars had brought Lauren and me together for five years, but they couldn't keep us together forever. I walked back to the house and upstairs to the bedroom. I was asleep within three minutes.

The next day at work I started wondering why New Jersey's nickname was the Garden State. I don't think that there are more gardens in New Jersey than in any other state. And then I remembered that the pharmaceutical nickname for New Jersey was the Biogarden. It got that nickname because there are so many pharmaceutical companies located in New Jersey. I liked the sound of that—I worked in the Biogarden state.

I did some research and found that—in terms of real farming—what New Jersey was known for were its cranberry farms, its horse farms, and its cornfields—New Jersey sweet corn is famous. I realized that between its farms and its Biogardens New Jersey was a biologist's paradise. With this is mind, I started formulating a new plan for my life. I wanted to become a self-supporting biologist not subject to the whimsical politics of pharmaceutical companies. Of course, I would have to start small and grow slowly.

Just envisioning this scheme for the rest of my life provided me what I was looking for—exaltation. I knew that if I was persistent—driven even—I could make this dream a reality. Cash flow would come from my pharmaceutical career, and I would grow my business slowly on the side. It might take decades, but this is what I wanted.

CHAPTER

I bought an acre of land just west of Princeton, New Jersey. On it, I was able to plant one hundred rows of vegetables. I planted ten rows each of corn, squash, pumpkins, green beans, lettuce, potatoes, broccoli, carrots, onions, and tomatoes. I planted in the spring, hoping for a late summer or fall harvest. If I could sell my produce, I would use the profits to buy more land.

All that summer I tended my field. I weeded each row by hand. I watered each row by hand. Then I poured my natural organic fertilizer on each row and also used natural plant food. I enjoyed my work. I came back to the farmhouse each night, my hands caked in dirt. I relished the sweat on my body and the dirt on my hands and knees. I also had a few cuts and scrapes. I cherished them. I was a bloody, dirty mess, but I felt exalted.

That summer, my evenings were filled with farming. I read every book I could get my hands on about farming. I was a voracious reader, and I digested everything I could get my hands on about farming.

Sometimes I think back with rue that I wasn't man enough for my ex-wife. Fortunately, farming took so much attention, it took away my ability to look back. There was only dirt, water, weeds, and plants. Since I couldn't make my marriage grow, I would compensate by making my plants grow.

That's actually all I owned in this world, a one-acre plot of land a few miles west of Princeton, New Jersey. Nestled in my two-centuries-old farmhouse, I felt like I was living in a chrysalis, hibernating, waiting to become something else. I didn't know what it was, but I knew it would be something better than I was now. The analogy from nature, of course, was a caterpillar about to become a butterfly.

I knew that it would be something lighter than I was now, something more sublime, a man without fetters. For after all, what is an unmarried man but an unchained creature, free from the shackles of a domestic life he probably never even wanted?

This country was founded on the freedom to choose—the freedom of religion—the freedom to pursue happiness in any way he sees fit—and the freedom to go where he wants when he wants. I finally started to value my freedom. I enjoyed my evenings alone. I gazed at the stars, especially Antares, and tended my garden until the sunset. Although it was a dull routine, it kept me satisfied and out of trouble.

I thought about George Orwell's solution for the down and out of society. He said that if they turned every shelter into a working farm, the shelter could become self-sufficient by supplying its own food, and instead of being idle, they would have work to do. I realized that I was living George Orwell's solution, except that I had a real job. In essence, though, even though I was making a lot of money, I felt down and out. My wife was gone, my home was gone, and I had experienced a form of down and out-hood. Nevertheless, after all, is said and done, I was starting to feel at peace with myself. I had tried my best to make my marriage work and had nothing to be ashamed of. As for poverty, I know that I hadn't experienced the ultimate depths of poverty. I was a learned man, the same thing that kept Orwell from experiencing the depths of poverty. All the workers at the shelters he stayed in still respected a man of learning temporarily down on his luck. In Britain, they called such a man a gentleman.

In the United States, there are more classes of the down and out. Whereas in Britain during Orwell's time there were only gentleman bums and a bum's bum, in the United States there are many different shades of bum. The classic railroad-riding bum with his five-day-old beard and tobacco-stained hands still exists in the United States, but they are a dying breed. The homeless in the United States is real. They are the ones who sleep on manhole covers for warmth and in the crevices of buildings in all of our major cities. There are shelters for them, but they are so down and out that they don't even think of using them. They are like wild animals on the loose. Half of them were deposited on the streets from psychiatric hospitals whose belt-

244 | GARRET GODWIN

tightening forced them out. Of the other half, half of them are schizophrenic but never sought treatment and went directly to the streets. The remaining one-quarter for the most part are just unlucky. Maybe they lost their job; maybe they went through a divorce—who knows. Sometimes these people wind up sleeping in their cars, and then when they sell their cars, they wind up on the street. That is the power that money has in our society today—it can either make you or break you.

There is still another class of down and out in America that needs to be talked about. There is a new phrase to describe them—"the working poor." These are the millions of people who hold minimum wage jobs or slightly better and still have a hard time making ends meet. A 40hour a week minimum wage job only brings you up to around the official poverty line. These Americans have enough to live on but not much more than that. They live a no-frills existence where even a vacation is too expensive an extravagance. There is nothing sadder to me than seeing a seventy-year-old working at Mcdonald's.

These then are the shades of the down and out in America—the railroad bums, the homeless, and the working poor. There are a few others as well, such as the "in-between" jobs like I was, but most of our down and outfit into one of the former three categories.

Our modern capitalistic society has so many pitfalls. Even in biblical times, it was said that money was the root of all evil. Two thousand years later, it couldn't be more true. Unfortunately, so much importance is put on money that people forget what's truly important in life. Over half of all divorces are over money issues. Women are genetically attracted to alpha males, who usually make more money than their Type B husbands. They drop their current mate for a better deal at the drop of a hat. I should know; it happened to me.

CHAPTER

As the summer months rolled on, and my vegetables grew, I started planning how I was going to market my produce. I decided to drive to Lancaster County, Pennsylvania, and visit an Amish farm. I drove to the heart of Lancaster County and stopped at a farm. I discovered foods, including chou chou, jalapena eggs, spiced pears, parmesan salad dressing, and pear butter. I thought to myself—what a great idea! The massive agricultural companies don't make specialty products anymore. Only the small independent farmers still sell products like these. The label on the bottles and jars said, "Jake & Amos," and there was a picture of two bearded men without mustaches and black Amish straw hats. They were both smiling. Actually, their products were more expensive than the mass-produced stuff you get in the grocery store, but their uniqueness made up for that. I drove back to Princeton with my bag of products.

I tended my garden trying to envision how my vegetables would look as finished products. I wanted to have a nice finished product, one with my own logo. I knew that if I had a recognizable logo, it would help to sell the product.

Perhaps there are better ways to make a living than by farming, but I can't think of any. My job in the pharmaceutical industry was good, but not really very rewarding. At least I was still on Dr. Feingold's good side. However, pharmaceuticals was a mercurial business, and I knew that his opinion of me could change at any time.

I think that I am becoming Franz Kafka. I have been thinking a lot about metamorphosis. I began to realize that I was currently in a pupa stage of my life—in a cocoon trying to become something better than I was now. In the insect world, this was called imaginal ecdysis—full transformation. Into what, I didn't know. All I knew is that it would be something wonderful.

I was in a cocoon right now. I realized that I had been spinning it ever since I arrived in Princeton. I was running every day, perfecting my body and tending my garden plot, which was spiritually healing. My mind was a honed weapon at work. After one has suffered a setback as I did, these are the three things that most deserve working on— the body, mind, and spirit.

After all, is said and done, this is all each one of us has to work with. No matter whether you're rich or poor, single or attached, employed or unemployed, in the end, we are only a soul and an intellect inhabiting a body. What we do with these tools determines our lives. We can use them to create great happiness and joy, or we can use them to create a life of misery. Even the best of us can still make colossal mistakes—that is part of being human. The trick is to keep learning from our mistakes. Each time we fall and get up again we are a little bit stronger.

Having gone through a divorce and a period of unemployment, I only got a little taste of what it means to be down and out. The world is constantly improving itself, and I can't help but think of the millions in past centuries who may have known nothing except poverty. This legacy continues into the present, but it is different now. Safety nets such as unemployment compensation and social security have saved millions from poverty. I think that this is just the beginning. Of course, I am just talking about this country. Many third-world countries are still centuries behind us. We need to help them catch up. We need some type of world anti-poverty program. Such programs are now just beginning to take shape. We already have a global economy. Perhaps within the next century, we will also have a world welfare system. In the meantime, maybe we should strive to be a little more sensitive to each other's needs. Programs like Habitat for Humanity can help the few, but we need new programs to help the many. We need to compete globally but think locally. We need a grassroots culture of caring. We need to overcome the every man for himself mentality that capitalism forces upon us. We are slowly getting there, but we are not there yet.

CPSIA information can be obtained
at www.ICGtesting.com
Printed in the USA
LVHW101649060922
727695LV00002B/217